MINDFULNESS BIBLE: 4 BOOKS IN 1:

BEGINNER'S COLLECTION FOR RELIEVING ANXIETY, STRESS AND DECLUTTERING YOUR MIND USING MEDITATION, MINIMALISM AND ESSENTIAL OILS

By
Beatrice Anahata

© **Copyright 2019 - All rights reserved.**

This document is geared towards providing exact and reliable information in regards to the topic and issue covered. The publication is sold with the idea that the publisher is not required to render accounting, officially permitted, or otherwise, qualified services. If advice is necessary, legal or professional, a practiced individual in the profession should be ordered.

- From a Declaration of Principles which was accepted and approved equally by a Committee of the American Bar Association and a Committee of Publishers and Associations.

In no way is it legal to reproduce, duplicate, or transmit any part of this document in either electronic means or in printed format. Recording of this publication is strictly prohibited and any storage of this document is not allowed unless with written permission from the publisher. All rights reserved.

The information provided herein is stated to be truthful and consistent, in that any liability, in terms of inattention or otherwise, by any usage or abuse of any policies, processes, or directions contained within is the solitary and utter responsibility of the recipient reader. Under no circumstances will any legal responsibility or blame be held against the publisher for any reparation, damages, or monetary loss due to the information herein, either directly or indirectly.

Respective authors own all copyrights not held by the publisher.

The information herein is offered for informational purposes solely, and is universal as so. The presentation of the information is without contract or any type of guarantee assurance.

The trademarks that are used are without any consent, and the publication of the trademark is without permission or backing by the trademark owner. All trademarks and brands within this book are for clarifying purposes only and are the owned by the owners themselves, not affiliated with this document.

Table of Contents

Book 1: Mindfulness for Beginners 9
Introduction 10
The Situation of It All.. 18
The Seven Forms Of Meditation Quick Guide......... 25
How to Fight Cravings with Mindfulness 29
Basic Techniques To Customize 33
Just A Final Recap.. 40
Some things to think about 42

Book 2: Mindfulness 49
Week One 50
Ways of Achieving Mindfulness in Everyday Life .. 51
Timing Mindfulness 56
The Pre-Test Mindful Day.. 62
DAY 1: Mindful Body Meditation 63
DAY 2: Mindful Breathing Meditation..................... 65
DAY 3: Mindful Sound Meditation 66
Day 4: Mindful Hand Meditation 68
Day 5: Mindful Head Meditation 69
Day 6: Mindful Sensation Meditation 70
Day 7: Just Be Meditation 71
Week 2 72
Day 8: Mindful Day.. 72
Day 9: Mindful Relaxing.. 74
Day 10: Mindful Conversations 75
Day 11: Mindfully Combat Negativity..................... 76
Day 12: Mindful Walking 78

Day 13: Mindful Commute 80
Day 14: Mindful Meals 82
Week Three 83
Day Fifteen 84
Day Sixteen 84
Day Seventeen 85
Day Eighteen 86
Day Nineteen 87
Day Twenty 87
Day Twenty-One 88
Week Four 89
Day Twenty-Two 89
Day Twenty-Three 90
Day Twenty-Four 90
Day Twenty-Five 91
Day Twenty-Six 91
Day Twenty-Seven 92
Day Twenty-Eight 92
Day Twenty-Nine 93
Day Thirty 93
What Exactly is Inner Peace? 95
How Chaotic Lifestyles Ruin Your Inner Peace and Happiness 99
Positive Characteristic Features of Mindfulness 108
The First Phase of Becoming Mindful 112
The Second Phase of Becoming Mindful 118
Ways of Sustaining Your Mindfulness in the Midst of Negativities 129
Conclusion 133

Book 3: Minimalist 135
Chapter 1: Minimalism 136
Get Down to Business 143
Thirty Days to Prepare 146
Where Is the Joy in All of This? 159
Chapter 2: Days 1 to 10 161
Chapter 3: Days 11 to 20 179
Chapter 4: Days 21 to 30 197
Book 4: Essential Oils 210
Do you like essential oils? 211
BASIC RECIPES 213
Acne 229
Aging Skin 231
Air Freshener 233
Anger 235
Anxiety 237
Arthritis 239
Asthma 241
Back Pain 244
Bathroom Care 246
Blisters 249
Bloating 251
Body Odor 253
Bronchitis 257
Bug Bites and Stings 259
Bug Repellent 262
Cellulite 265
Chapped Lips 268
Chilblains 270

Colds and Flu 272
Colic 275
Conjunctivitis 277
Cough 279
Cradle Cap 281
Cuts and Scrapes 282
Diaper Rash 285
Diarrhea 287
Ear Infection 289
Eczema 291
Fatigue 293
Fever 296
Flatulence 299
More Recipes 306
Conclusion 348

Before you sit down to read this book, I want you to really understand what you are getting yourself into. This is a life changing process. You will learn a lot about who you are and who you want to be. You may see a shift in your priorities. You may see some things are not really priorities. My goal is not to change the world. My goal is to help you find out who you are.

"When you realize nothing is lacking, the whole world belongs to you." ~Lao Tzu

Book 1: Mindfulness for Beginners

32 easy mindfulness exercises for beginners on how to live life in the present moment, relieve stress and reduce anxiety.

By Beatrice Anahata

Introduction

mind·ful·ness

ˈmīn(d)f(ə)lnəs/

noun

1.

the quality or state of being conscious or aware of something.

"their mindfulness of the wider cinematic tradition"

2.

a mental state achieved by focusing one's awareness on the present moment, while calmly acknowledging and accepting one's feelings, thoughts, and bodily sensations, used as a therapeutic technique.

Getting Started

Life is busy. We have a million things on our to do list, plus another list that doesn't seem to make it to the to do list. Whether you have children, a partner, a full-time job, or it just feels like your life has seemed to slip away from you, meditation can help. Life is overwhelming. It's easy to lose focus. Your mind gets cloudy. Before you know it, it seems like you are just drifting. So now let's get our footing back.

I have to tell you about your room. Right now, it is blank. There isn't anything in there. For the first couple of times, you will need to count to 100 to reach the state of mind that is considered your room. It will be bland. It will be without much to look out, missing colors, and even decorations. Each time that you go, I will point out other things for you to look at and see. Eventually, you will be able to fill in the blanks. Your staircase will change. It may be shorter. There may be a hand rail. Colors will change. Your door may change. You may get to that state of mind one day and you have a pet. You may get there one day and the colors are bright and welcoming. It is your subconscious. It is all about who you are. Let it be. I will say that a lot. Let it be. Why? Because it isn't worth changing. Sometimes you just have to take things as they come. So your two year old wants to wear snow boots in 100 degree weather. Let it be. Just carry shoes with you for when they peel them off. Focus on what you can change. Focus on what you want to change. Only then can you truly be mindful.

The first thing you have to learn is who you are. You need to know what your fears are. You have to know where you are losing your confidence. This first exercise is about self-awakening. I want you to take the time to really focus. Find you a quiet spot. Don't lie down. You will likely fall asleep. Be inspired. If you can't write it out, draw it out. If you do fall asleep, write down your dream as soon as you wake up.

There is no such thing as a failed attempt to mindfulness – just a lack of practice.

Exercise # 1: Facing Who You are

Close your eyes. Take a deep breath. In through your nose and out through your mouth. Imagine in front of your there is a set of stairs. At the top of the stairs in a door. Picture that door. What does it look like? Focus on it as you climb the stairs. Each step you take count. When you get to 100 you should be at the top of the stairs. Welcome to your room. This is your room. Everything about it is your creation. This room holds your happiness, your fears, and even your sadness. There is no stress. There is no judgment. This is all about you. In your room there are three very important things. One is a desk. This is where you will sit and write. You can process everything and nothing just by sitting here. As you focus on your desk, your room will come alive before you. You will notice things about you that you hadn't noticed before. Your desk has drawers. The things stored there are feelings and memories that you have had and haven't wanted to let go off. These control your daily life. You have an unlimited supply of paper and all your favorite writing tools. As you write you will discover the things that you hadn't wanted to face. It's not scary. There is no one here to judge you. It's time to face those fears. Write them. Focus on what you are hiding from yourself. You are in control here. When you are done writing, get up and go to the door. Take each step slowly as you count down from 100.

So, what was this? This was you facing things you didn't want to face. You should have learned more about who you are. Maybe the stress of that day you yelled at your child has been weighing on your heart. Maybe you aren't sure if you are making the right career path. I suggest that you take the time to write this all down. It is definitely going to come pouring out. Release those fears on to your notebook paper. Let them shine. Realize them for what they are or you will never be able to get away from them. It is time for you to be mindful of what you fear so that you can change them.

Exercise #2: The quick trip tip

Let me explain that this is something that you have to do every day but you really need to do it at least once a week or so. It takes ten minutes tops. You can do it quicker or you can take longer but average it to ten minutes.

Close your eyes. Count to ten. Clear your mind completely and totally. Now. Open them and write. Write everything that crosses your mind. Don't think. Don't worry. Definitely don't organize. Just write it all down. When you are finished. Read it. Think about it. Is what you wrote things you can change? Are they things that you want to change? Are they really worth stressing and worrying yourself over?

You need to learn that there will always be things that you will worry about that you just can't change. These are things that, through meditation, you will learn to let go. This is a learning process. You will have to constantly make readjustments to your thinking. That's why it is called the train of thought, because it will stay on the right track, but once you switch the direction, it can be impossible to get back on the right track to your destination. Don't give up, just readjust.

I don't know about you, but for the longest time when I thought of people meditating, I thought about some barely dressed person sitting on a towel with their legs entwined and their fingers touching. It was completely and totally intimidating. I thought, ummm no. I am slightly overweight. I am short. I don't think I want to be half naked on the floor. I will look like a blob. Not to mention, I just am not that religious, so it has to be a complete waste of time. BUTTTTTTTT let me tell you something, just please never tell anyone: I WAS WRONG. Yep. Me. I don't admit it often.

What was I wrong about?

1. You don't need to be half naked to find yourself – duh.

2. You don't need to assume any certain position.

3. You don't have to sit on the floor.

4. You don't even need a towel.

5. YOU DO NOT HAVE TO BE LOOKING FOR GOD.

Don't get me wrong. You will find meditation in just about any and every religion. Christian bibles tell you to meditate on the Word of God so that you can engrain them in your heart. Buddhism will tell you to that meditation will lead you to a road of enlightenment. So, what does this teach us? That 1) if you really want something to be a part of you, meditate on it 2) that if you meditate, you will find your path.

Speaking of path, that brings me to:

Exercise #3: The path

Here I am not talking about what person to date. I am talking about life changing decisions that will ultimately guide you to where you need to be. It's like choosing between that job in California and the one in New York. It is the twisting turning, they both have good sides, path.

Count to ten. Take deep steady breaths. Imagine in front of you are the woods. With each and every step, you are deeper in the woods. At ten, STOP. Look around. You see two paths you can take. One path looks bright and sunny. The other path looks shady and cool. Pick on and take a walk down it. Keep your mind clear. Just focus on your steps. The smells of the woods are around you. Enjoy your journey. Each step brings you closer to your destiny. When you get to the end of your path, what do you see? Write it down. Which one of your choices does it resemble the most?

Exercise #4: Imagining your life

Take a minute. Focus on what you love about your life right now. Think about all the things you never want to change. What do you love about your house?

Your routine? Now think about one of your options. How will those things change? How will that become better? What will come worse? Now, thing about your other choice. Ask yourself the same questions. Do you see the clear difference?

I always tend to go to the method 4 when I am really wanting a change for the better. I always get stuck in a routine that gets boring. On the other hand, change can be downright terrifying. These steps help to take the guesswork out of it and help to solidify what I need to do so that I can do it with no issues. A little peace of mind goes a long way.

The Situation of It All

Here is the crazy thing about life. It is always the most stressful in short bursts that make you wonder if you are going to lose your mind before you manage to get through it. These short bursts sometimes only last minutes or hours. By the end of the day, or maybe the week, everything comes into perspective and you realize it wasn't so bad after all. So now I will take the time to go over some situations that seem so very bad and show you how to be **MINDFUL** of your temporary situation so that you make it through without falling apart.

So here you are at the grocery store. You really only wanted to pick up a few things and be on your way. So you make your way to the register and there is that woman there. You know which one I am talking about. The one with two basket full of groceries. She has a one screaming kid and one kid going through the candy like it has never eaten before. It is the only register open. Then just when you think it's almost over, she pulls out her coupon book. The manager gets called over to take her complaint and you really want to just scream. However you could just use:

Exercise #5:

Take a deep breath. Slowly count. If the kid hears you, they will probably get out of the candy, but don't focus on that. Just count your breaths. Think to yourself, be peaceable with all mankind. In and out. You will feel your mind clear. You will see the light at the end of the tunnel. Just like that and your aisle is clear. See, that wasn't so bad, now was it?

Sitting at your desk at work. Your desk is piled up with a million papers for you to look at. You have an inbox that will take you until lunch to get through. There is a meeting after lunch. You have no idea how you are going to get it all done. So how about:

Exercise #6:

Stop what you are doing and breath. Picture yourself in an empty field. Imagine the wind blowing. Count up to 100. Say to yourself: I am at peace. This is no big deal. Feel the tension relax out of your body. Clear mind. Clear body. Keep counting until you find all your stress just go away.

It has been a long day. The kids are running around everywhere. You just want to stop and relax. It seems like the more stressful day you have a work, the more there is to do at home. It never stops. However:

Exercise #7:

can help you to reset your mind. All you have to do is stop. Sit down. Calmly begin to count. You can count out loud if you would like. Your kids may need a quick reset. So just count. Breath steady and clearly. Stop counting when you feel your mind reset and your body relax. You are now ready to continue.

You are late. You forgot to set your alarm, or maybe you turned it off in your sleep. Either way, you are definitely not going to make it to your shift on time. And now you are stuck in traffic. As far as you can see there is nothing but tail lights. So you could scream – it won't do any good. Or you could do:

Exercise #8:

Turn on some classical music. It is always calming. Don't close your eyes. It would be not so smart while you are driving. Just focus your energy on relaxing. Count to 100. Take steady, even breaths. Focus on releasing the stress out of your soul. Feel your mind clearing. Feel you mind preparing for a positive day.

You are balancing your checking account. You definitely don't see how you are going to make it. The stress of the bills are weighing you down. You can try:

Exercise #9:

Think about what you want to accomplish. Visualize it and focus on it. Imagine your bank account balancing. Clear your mind. Feel the stress melt away. You will see that it will all come together. A plan will form and your stress will go away.

Social anxiety sucks. It is so hard to deal with. You want to go out. You want people to like you, but you just can't get past the inability to breathe. Your palms get sweaty. You feel like you don't make any sense. Overall, you are just plain awkward. You have gone over all the conversation starters you can possibly think of, but nothing sounds natural. So it is time for:

Exercise #10:

Take a deep breath. Listen to your heart. Know who you are. Think of all the great things you have to offer to the conversation. Count back from 20 and feel the anxiety roll away. Before you know it, you are a new person. You are ready for the conversation. Jump in and don't be afraid of the silence from time to time.

It is time to cram for that test. You are on your third pot of coffee and none of the information is sticking. Your eyes just want to close. Don't give up yet. I know a technique that may help you. I had a friend that swore he could write things on his chalkboard and never forget them. So here is:

Exercise #11:

Close your eyes. Take a deep breath. In through your nose and out through your mouth. Imagine in front of your there is a set of stairs. At the top of the stairs in a door. Picture that door. What does it look like? Focus on it as you climb the stairs. Each step you take count. When you get to 100 you should be at the top of the stairs. Welcome to your room. This is your room. Everything about it is your creation. This room holds your happiness, your fears, and even your sadness. There is no stress. There is no judgment. This is all about you. In your room there are three very important things. One is a desk. You already know about the desk so we are going to ignore it for now. Look at your walls. There is a chalkboard on one of them. Visualize yourself writing on this chalkboard. Picture each and every word as you write it. This will ingrain it into your memory. Write down all the important things that you know you will need for your exam. Make charts. Keep it simple. You will see that it will all come together. When you are finished, you will feel more confident and prepared for your exam.

While you are in your room, look at the bookcase behind you. It is massive. It takes up the entire wall. On it is every book you ever wrote. Each book is a year of your life. Some of the books are thick, they contain life experiences. They lay out exactly what you think you learned from that experience. Take the time to look them over. You may find that you overlooked a lesson. Now, count back from 100 and return to your life. Feel refreshed and ready to face the world.

I would love to tell you all about my room. I would love to tell you the details. The colors that come to life when I visit it. I cannot. I do not want to influence your room. I want you to create it yourself. So, please enjoy it.

Meditation is amazing. It is an amazing tool. I hope that you can use these to get through some common stresses at the very moment that you are going through them. I think that it would help you to better understand that you are dealing with temporary problems. Your life can change dramatically from one minute to the next. Next year will be completely different, so don't focus on anything other than right now. Make each and every moment stress free. You are the only one that can do this. Only you can control what worries you. My mom always told me, don't stress over the apple pie burning when you know you are going to be enjoying the smell of it all through the house. It means, why worry about something when you know you are doing the best that you can to make sure that it never turns out that way. Life is hard enough without stressing over every detail.

The Seven Forms Of Meditation Quick Guide

Transcendental Meditation – Exercise #12

You will see this among the traditional Hindu. So this is basically chanting your way over the stress. You repeat the same mantra over and over again until you achieve a higher state of mind. You want to place the negative aspects at the bottom and rise above it. The easiest way to do this is to download a video. You can do it as a beginner, but it isn't as easy. I highly suggest this if you are a hands on type of learner because you have to focus your mind to repeat the words exactly so that they begin to consume you completely. It is a thing of beauty once you master it. It does take lots of practice. You should start of doing this out loud, which is fine in the car, but will get you some strange looks at work. Your kids probably wouldn't notice or think you are losing your mind, but that's okay.

Heart Rhythm Meditation – Exercise #13

I don't suggest this to beginners. It is the focus of the heart rhythm in order to guide you to a higher state of mind. You have to really focus on your heart and allow your breathing to sync with it. It can be quite difficult to achieve, but if you do, it is the ultimate in soul awakening experiences. You will find that you are happier when you learn to do it regularly. It is a whole body experience.

Kundalini – Exercise #14

is just a little bit different than all the rest. It is really simple. All you really need to do is focus on the very center of your body. Concentrate until you find the core of your breathing. Feel your stress uncoiling from there and floating to the outside of your body. You want to literally feel your stress rising up out of the center of your body and leaving you completely and totally. You will feel lighter. You will feel more free. You may even find who you are.

Guided Visualization – Exercise #15

This may not be what you are looking for if you are reading this book. Let me tell you why. You have to have the visual. You need to be walked through each and every step. Listen to a recording of yourself being guided through visualizing your problems away. It is time consuming. I don't like it. I don't even know if I like it being number 16. The reason it is listed is because it is real. It can help you, but you cannot do it on your own. It isn't a quick fix. It will lead you to self awareness, destress you, and make you happy. Just make sure you get a voice that you like to hear the sound of, or record yourself and listen to it later. That would make it easier for you, maybe. I just know that this one is not for me.

Qi Gong – Exercise #16

This exercise comes from the Chinese idea that all your body systems are connected. It is called the whole body approach to health. It is directed at releasing negative energy so that your body can heal itself. A stressed body is a sick body. Your focus needs to be on breathing techniques. You want to breath and direct energy to each part of your body. It will sync your healing so that your stress is released and your mind is clear which will allow your energy to focus on healing your body. It is so simple. You just deep breath and focus on your aches and relax them. Your body will feel energized.

Zazen – Exercise #17

This is the Zen method borrowed from Buddha. You are supposed to sit in the legs crossed position in the floor to keep your energy flowing in the circle of your body. You want to sit with your legs crossed and your hands in your lap. You need to focus all your thoughts into releasing the negative ideas, comments, and thoughts from your head completely. You should focus on breathing until you feel released and free. At first, it may be difficult to achieve that perfect peace quickly, but as you practice, you will get there quicker and quicker.

Traditional Western – Exercise #18

The thing is that this is where mindfulness comes from. It is simple. It is teaching your mind to refocus off the negativity and refocus on its ability to find the good in the situation. It encompasses all forms of meditation. It is the simple calming of your spirit to enjoy who you are. Simple deep breathing to readjust your train of thought. It is taking five minutes to reorganize your priorities. It is loving yourself. Just breath until you feel settled.

How to Fight Cravings with Mindfulness

Fight Cravings – Exercise #19

No matter what you are trying to do, or not do, mindfulness can help. You can calm your craving for a cigarette. You can break your addiction to food. There are many ways to use The very second that you feel your craving coming on, focus on it. Feel the craving in your body. Feel the tingle. Feel the ability to fight it. It is real. It is a chemical part of your body. Now focus on it. Make up your mind that your ultimate outcome is far more beneficial than giving into this single craving. Allow it to dissolve. Release it from your body. You will begin to notice that space between cravings is getting bigger. Soon they will be gone altogether. You can do this.

Awaken Your Senses – Exercise #20

Are you feeling bad? Do you feel sluggish and want a new outlook? Let's try to awaken your senses. You may be surprised at how much better you can feel from this simple I want you to find somewhere quiet. Light a candle. Now. Let's start with your sense of smell. I want you to think about exactly how that candle smells. What are the other scents in the room? Can you smell anything outside of the room? Taste. Can you taste the scent of the candle? What does it remind you of? Touch. Can you feel the heat off the candle? Does it add to the taste? Does it take away from the taste? Hear. What sounds can you hear that the candle makes you think of? How does it tie in with the taste, touch, and smell of the room around you? Finally, what can you see in your mind's eye that brings everything home? What has this experience taught you about who you are? What has it taught you about the world around you? How can you use this in your mindful meditation later? This is all about reopening your senses because we tend to shut them down and get tunnel vision.

Sleep Better – Exercise #21

Now let's use mindfulness to help you to fight your insomnia and stay asleep so that your body can reach REM state. Without that precious REM state, your body cannot rejuvenate. Lay down. Focus on your breathing. Concentrate on how your abdomen muscles expand with each breath. Imagine your breath coming out your mouth. In with your nose. Steady pattern. Regular breathing is a must. Now focus on your toes. Wiggle them slightly. Release the tension in them. Move up your legs. Release the stress in them. Move through your body. Focus on each part. Release the stress from each pocket. Find the stress points and gently massage them with your mind. If your mind begins to wander to current events in your life, gently refocus it and bring it back to where it was. It is all about relaxing and letting the day go. Every time that you exhale, release the stress out with the bad air. You can do this every night. Soon your body will be trained to let everything go as soon as you lay in bed at night. Your sleepless nights are soon to be a thing of the past. Remember to try to keep a dream journal when you wake up in the morning. Dreams are just your subconscious trying to tell you something or release the drama in your life. You would be surprised at the power of your dreams in your daily life. Keeping track of them will help you to find your way if you are feeling lost or confused – but that is for another book at another time.

Controlling Your Thoughts and Emotions – Exercise #22

I know that this is the hardest part of life. It isn't easy to control your judgment of your own thoughts. I know that sounds weird, but we are our biggest enemy. We hold ourselves back. is all about thinking about what your mind wants to think about. Just letting thoughts flow. Sit in a way that you will feel comfortable.

Focus on just breathing, such as the feeling of the air flowing into your nose and out through your mouth. Once you have focused your concentration fully. Focus on your thoughts. Become aware of sounds, sensations, and ideas within your own head.

Let each thought flow without deciding if it is good or bad. If your thoughts flow to fast refocus your breathing. Then begin all over again.

Let me think. We covered common stressful situations. We have covered tricks to help common problems. I have compartmentalized the absolute best that I could. So I guess now I can just give you the techniques. These are basics that can cover anything. They can be completely personalized. They can handle whatever you want. They are the basics.

Basic Techniques To Customize

Deep Breathing – Exercise #23

Deep breathing is taking slow, deep, methodical mouthfuls of air and slow exhalations. You can do it for as you want to. If your mind wanders simply try to refocus on your breathing.

- Inhale through your nose.
- Feel your breath travel down into your stomach. Feel your lungs expand.
- Focus on the ambiences of breathing deeply and slowly.
- You will be able to feel your body rise and fall on each draw of your breath.

Doing a Seated Meditation – Exercise #24

Find a quiet spot. You can meditate anywhere. However, you will probably want to be somewhere you won't be distracted. You want somewhere comfortable. Even if that is just closing the door to your office. You could just take a walk to a nearby park or library.

- Turn off all your electronics just to keep them from bothering.

- Give yourself 5 or ten minutes. Get comfortable. You just need a position that will help you to relax.
- When you're comfortable close your eyes.
- Focus on your breath. Block out any other thoughts. Any time you find your mind wandering, simply return your focus.
- Take deep breaths that go all the way down to your abdomen.
- Feel the air flow through your nostrils and into your lungs.
- Notice the feeling of your chest rising and falling with each inhalation and exhalation.
- You can set a timer for 5 to 10 minutes, but I prefer to breathe until I feel a sense of peace come over me.
- You can take these little meditation breaks anytime you want to.
- Open your eyes. When you're finished, slowly open your eyes. Don't get up right away. Just give your mind time to readjust to the peace.
- Stand up slowly.

Visualization Meditation – Exercise # 25

Get relaxed and breathe intensely. Use deep breathing exercises, just like you have already learned in the rest of the book.

Sit in a quiet spot and remove as many distractions as you can. Turn off your cellphone and find somewhere you can be alone just for a few minutes.

- ☯ Release any tight clothing.
- ☯ You can visualize whatever you want. It can be a real place you have been, or your own imaginary world. Really focus so that your mind thinks it is there.
- ☯ Start by picturing a visual image in your head. Choose a place that is totally relaxing. Think of all the things that you imagine would make the place peaceful.
- ☯ Imagine the sounds you'd hear there.
- ☯ Next, imagine the physical sensations you might experience there.
- ☯ Open your eyes and stand up slowly.

Mindful Observation – Exercise #26

This exercise is unassuming but unbelievably influential. It is designed to all us to connect us with the natural environment, which is so easy for us to forget to do on a regular basis.

Choose an ordinary object from your direct atmosphere and focus on watching it. This could be a living thing like a flower or your child or even just the clouds in the sky.

Don't do anything else. Focus on only the thing you are looking at. Simply relax into a peaceful state for as long as you possibly can. Look at it as if you have never seen it before.. Visually explore every part of its being. Let it take over your mind completely and totally. Connect with its energy and purpose in your world.

Mindful Awareness – Exercise #27

Think of something that you do every day, more than once a day. Or focus on something that happens several times throughout the day. It should be something that you sometimes forget to notice or take for granted that will always be there. Like maybe the refrigerator light.

Think about how much harder life would be without it. Or doorknobs, what would you do without them? What would a door look like? It makes you really appreciate the little things in life. Change it every day. Like maybe the smell of you cooking can remind you to be thankful that you have food to cook or children to feed. Or when you notice your spouse forgot to get gas, redirect that thought and be thankful you have the vehicle that needs gas.

Mindful Listening – Exercise #28

Pick a song that you have never heard before. It could be on the radio or maybe just something on your playlist that you haven't listened to yet. Close your eyes. Put in your ear-buds. Listen to the song. Even if you don't really like it at first, just listen. All your soul to reach down into the song and feel the beat. Let it consume your mind until you feel like you are one with the music.

Mindful Immersion – Exercise #29

Through yourself into a task. It doesn't matter what it is. Just give yourself over to it completely. If it is cleaning the floor, then just focus on appreciating the way that it looks clean. Appreciate the way that the sun shines on it. Appreciate the colors in it. The beauty of it. If you do this then your daily routines won't seem so routine any more.

Mindful Appreciation #30

Find five things that you are thankful for. I do it every night before I go to bed. It really helps to melt away the stress and the headaches. You could stop every time you are frustrated and find five reason why you love your life. You can look around your messy house and find five reasons why you love the mess. You can look at your spouse who won't decide what to have for dinner and just start telling them the five reasons that you love them. It is all about refocusing on who you are and why you love your life. It is about living in the moment.

Mindful brushing –Exercise #31

Sometimes we just get caught up in the routine of it all. We move through the motions, like when we brush or teeth or hair. Our mind will wonder and we will start to think about our worries, regrets, hopes, and fears. But what if you could take that time and refocus it in to a happy place? I want you to just focus on the art of brushing your teeth. Notice how it feels. Notice how it tastes. Really focus on that experience. It is a human experience. It is one we take for granted.

The Eating Exercise –Exercise #32

This is to bring your mind to what is right in front of you. You can pick any food you want. It is just a focus item. I want you to notice how it looks. Take in every single bump, curve, texture. Notice how it really feels, smooth, rough, and everything in between. How does it move when you touch it. Notice how the skin gives a little. Or how it doesn't give at all. Notice the smell. Then the taste. Focus on it totally and completely.

Just A Final Recap

I want to remind you that this is a journey that is all about you. It isn't about me. It isn't about your neighbor. It is about rediscovering what you love about your life. Mindfulness can help in so many ways.

It can

- Help you to de-stress
- Help you to realize your full potential
- Help you to realize your dreams
- Help you to reach your goals
- Help you to break addictions
- Help you to feel better

It cannot

- Change who you are at your core
- Change the people around you
- Change your situation
- Change your environment

I STRONGLY urge you to try all the techniques until you find one that you love. It is about you being happy. You will absolutely find what you are looking for, if it is within you. You won't get rich, but you may find it easier to manage money. It can't make your boss promote you, but it can give you an attitude change that may help you earn that promotion. It is about finding yourself. So please take time to focus on yourself. Love yourself first.

Some things to think about

I am including some quotes because sometimes you need something inspiring to really think about. I hope that you find one that really speaks to you and can help your center when everything else is falling apart. My favorite quote came from a TV show " Saved by the Bell" when I was 11 years old. I still tell myself this every single time I think about giving up. Now, I will tell you my trials have deepened over the years but this one quote has grown with me and changed meanings many times throughout the years. "Put your mind to it, go for, get down and break a sweat. Rock and Roll, You ain't seen nothing yet"

Here are some classics:

- Drink your tea slowly and reverently, as if it is the axis on which the world earth revolves – slowly, evenly, without rushing toward the future; live the actual moment. Only this moment is life." ~Thich Nhat Hanh."
- "As soon as we wish to be happier, we are no longer happy." ~Walter Landor
- "Mindfulness is the aware, balanced acceptance of the present experience. It isn't more complicated than that. It is opening to or receiving the present moment, pleasant or

unpleasant, just as it is, without either clinging to it or rejecting it." ~Sylvia Boorstein
- "The best way to capture moments is to pay attention. This is how we cultivate mindfulness. Mindfulness means being awake. It means knowing what you are doing." ~Jon Kabat-Zinn
- "In today's rush, we all think too much — seek too much — want too much — and forget about the joy of just being." ~Eckhart Tolle
- "If you want others to be happy, practice compassion. If you want to be happy, practice compassion." ~Dalai Lama
- "Suffering usually relates to wanting things to be different than they are." ~Allan Lokos
- "If we learn to open our hearts, anyone, including the people who drive us crazy, can be our teacher." ~Pema Chodron
- "If the doors of perception were cleansed, everything would appear to man as it is, infinite." ~William Blake
- "Feelings come and go like clouds in a windy sky. Conscious breathing is my anchor." ~Thich Nhat Han
- "If you want to conquer the anxiety of life, live in the moment, live in the breath." ~Amit Ray
- "In the end, just three things matter: How well we have lived. How well we have loved. How well we have learned to let go" ~Jack Kornfield

- "Do every act of your life as though it were the last act of your life." ~Marcus Aurelius
- "Everything is created twice, first in the mind and then in reality." ~Robin S. Sharma
- "Don't believe everything you think. Thoughts are just that – thoughts." ~Allan Lokos
- "Respond; don't react. Listen; don't talk. Think; don't assume." ~Raji Lukkoor
- "In this moment, there is plenty of time. In this moment, you are precisely as you should be. In this moment, there is infinite possibility." ~Victoria Moran
- "Mindfulness is simply being aware of what is happening right now without wishing it were different; enjoying the pleasant without holding on when it changes (which it will); being with the unpleasant without fearing it will always be this way (which it won't)." ~James Baraz
- "Mindfulness isn't difficult, we just need to remember to do it." ~Sharon Salzberg
- "It's only when we truly know and understand that we have a limited time on earth – and that we have no way of knowing when our time is up – that we will begin to live each day to the fullest, as if it was the only one we had." ~Elisabeth Kübler-Ross
- "Begin at once to live, and count each separate day as a separate life." ~Seneca

- "Today, like every other day, we wake up empty and frightened. Don't open the door to the study and begin reading. Take down a musical instrument." ~Rumi
- "I wish that life should not be cheap, but sacred. I wish the days to be as centuries, loaded, fragrant." ~Ralph Waldo Emerson
- "Each morning we are born again. What we do today is what matters most." ~Buddha
- "Always hold fast to the present. Every situation,indeed every moment,is of infinite value,for it is the representative of a whole eternity." ~Johann Wolfgang von Goethe
- "The way to live in the present is to remember that 'This too shall pass.' When you experience joy, remembering that 'This too shall pass' helps you savor the here and now. When you experience pain and sorrow, remembering that 'This too shall pass' reminds you that grief, like joy, is only temporary." ~Joey Green
- "If you concentrate on finding whatever is good in every situation, you will discover that your life will suddenly be filled with gratitude, a feeling that nurtures the soul." ~Rabbi Harold Kushner
- "There's only one reason why you're not experiencing bliss at this present moment, and it's because you're thinking or focusing on what you don't have…. But, right now you have

everything you need to be in bliss." ~Anthony de Mello

- "Our own worst enemy cannot harm us as much as our unwise thoughts. No one can help us as much as our own compassionate thoughts." ~Buddha
- "Observe the space between your thoughts, then observe the observer." ~Hamilton Boudreaux
- "The practice of mindfulness begins in the small, remote cave of your unconscious mind and blossoms with the sunlight of your conscious life, reaching far beyond the people and places you can see." ~Earon Davis
- "Life is not lost by dying; life is lost minute by minute, day by dragging day, in all the small uncaring ways." ~Stephen Vincent Benet
- "As long as we have practiced neither concentration nor mindfulness, the ego takes itself for granted and remains its usual normal size, as big as the people around one will allow." ~Ayya Khema
- "Impermanence is a principle of harmony. When we don't struggle against it, we are in harmony with reality." ~Pema Chodron
- The basic root of happiness lies in our minds; outer circumstances are nothing more than adverse or favorable." ~Matthieu Ricard

- "The mind in its natural state can be compared to the sky, covered by layers of cloud which hide its true nature." ~Kalu Rinpoche
- "Be kind whenever possible. It is always possible." ~Dalai Lama
- "If one were truly aware of the value of human life, to waste it blithely on distractions and the pursuit of vulgar ambitions would be the height of confusion." ~Dilgo Khyentse Rinpoche
- "Knowledge does not mean mastering a great quantity of different information, but understanding the nature of mind. This knowledge can penetrate each one of our thoughts and illuminate each one of our perceptions." ~Matthieu Ricard
- "The most precious gift we can offer others is our presence. When mindfulness embraces those we love, they will bloom like flowers." ~Thich Nhat Hanh
- "We are awakened to the profound realization that the true path to liberation is to let go of everything." ~Jack Kornfield
- "To diminish the suffering of pain, we need to make a crucial distinction between the pain of pain, and the pain we create by our thoughts about the pain. Fear, anger, guilt, loneliness and helplessness are all mental and emotional responses that can intensify pain." ~Howard Cutler

- "Things falling apart is a kind of testing and also a kind of healing." ~Pema Chodron
- "Why, if we are as pragmatic as we claim, don't we begin to ask ourselves seriously: Where does our real future lie?" ~Sogyal Rinpoche
- "Envy and jealousy stem from the fundamental inability to rejoice at someone else's happiness or success." ~Matthieu Ricard
- "By breaking down our sense of self-importance, all we lose is a parasite that has long infected our minds. What we gain in return is freedom, openness of mind, spontaneity, simplicity, altruism: all qualities inherent in happiness." ~Matthieu Ricard
- "Our lives are lived in intense and anxious struggle, in a swirl of speed and aggression, in competing, grasping, possessing and achieving, forever burdening ourselves with extraneous activities and preoccupations." ~Sogyal Rinpoche
- "Mindful and creative, a child who has neither a past, nor examples to follow, nor value judgments, simply lives, speaks and plays in freedom." ~Arnaud Desjardins
- "We have only now, only this single eternal moment opening and unfolding before us, day and night." Jack Kornfield

Book 2: Mindfulness

How to completely destroy stress and anxiety in 30 days

By

Beatrice Anahata

Week One

Week one will focus solely on meditation. Developing a meditation practice will help you develop mindfulness skills you can then apply in everyday situations. After week 1, there will not be any specific meditations laid out in the challenge but you are encouraged to continue incorporating a daily meditation practice into your weeks.

The daily meditations will focus on being mindful for a period of time yet each one will be slightly different. You may find some are easier, others are challenging, and some feel more comfortable for you. Going forward, you will have all the different types of meditation in your toolbox and can choose which ones you want to use. You decide each day how long you will meditate. Remember to start small. Once you feel you can be mindful for the entire duration of the meditation, increase the amount of time by a few minutes each practice. Remember that certain days will be better than others. The key is to not judge yourself; it is all part of the growing process. Let's get started!

Ways of Achieving Mindfulness in Everyday Life

In this chapter, we will explore ways of developing mindfulness while carrying out normal daily activities without the need for preset exercises. This may be helpful, as there are many situations in everyday life that lend themselves to impromptu mindful exercises. Therefore, in this chapter we will be looking at the many moments we have during the day, which can add to the exercises in the chapters which are to follow, simply by changing the way we do things and the way we behave.

If you wish, before you continue reading, pause for a moment and think about the many daily activities you do without ever really experiencing them to the full. Do take your time to think about these moments. Should you feel the need, you may also make a list of these moments.

Done? Surely you have come up with a rather long list of activities which most of us do automatically, we do them but pay no attention to them.

Here are some examples which may help you, in case you have not personally thought of these:

We often eat and drink without paying any attention whatsoever to what we are eating or drinking. We will have a whole chapter dedicated to these two activities, as eating and drinking mindfully is very important indeed, for many reasons.

We often walk around without even feeling that we are walking. Instead, walking is an activity which lends itself to developing mindfulness. Instead of focusing on the end of your journey, even if you are just popping round the corner to buy some groceries, why don't you focus on your body? You can choose any part of your body, though it may be a good idea to start with your feet.

Whilst you are walking on the sidewalk, feel the pressure of your soles on the ground; feel your foot lifting and leaving the ground, then feel how your whole leg moves following your foot, feel how your other foot holds your weight when you have lifted your foot... Focus your attention on and focus on your movement rather than on what you will be doing when you reach the store.

We often meet many people in our daily lives, to whom we pay very little or no attention at all. We simply exchange a polite word or a glance, but we do not really interact. This happens on a regular basis. In fact, this includes most of the people we meet every day. Instead, when you meet people on the street, try to feel their presence. If you see someone coming your way on the sidewalk, instead of just avoiding him or her, try to feel his or her very presence coming towards you.

You can do this in many ways: you can feel their heat next to yours, you can feel their emotions as they brush past you. If you are commuting, you may find yourself in close proximity with many people, most people find this an irritating experience, this is because we feel that they are "invading our space". However, this is just our ego talking, and making us feel "threatened" even if we know quite well that there is nothing to fear. Instead of trying to create a barrier and instead of trying to be as separate from them as you can possibly be, forget yourself for a moment and share your space with them.

However, feeling their body heat is often regarded as either annoying or embarrassing. But, think about how the very same sensation is pleasurable when the body heat comes from someone you love. Remember that in the end, they cannot cool down just because they are on a carriage, right next to you. Thus, instead of trying to avoid the inevitable, allow their heat to warm your skin, feel their heat warm your muscles and feel it without attaching any judgement to it.

Another thing people find irritating when commuting is body odor. Ok, you may not like everybody's smell, but there is very little you can do when you are commuting to and from work or school.

Instead of trying to avoid, or ignore such smell, which in the end is only natural, why don't you try to appreciate it? By appreciating, here we do not mean that you have to analyze it like a wine taster describes the bouquet of a glass of vintage Brunello di Monatalcino, but simply experience it for what it is. Experience it with your senses and let your senses do the thinking, instead of preconceived concepts such as bitterness, sweetness or likability and dis-likability.

Whenever you experience physical contact, do not shy away from it, even if it is just the brush of someone's hand, while you pay for your bread at the store. This happens often, so instead of feeling useless embarrassment, feel the person's hand touching yours, its warmth, the moistness of their skin, its texture, and allow it to speak to you, to share with you a sensation to which you need attach no value or judgement.

There are many other moments when we live our lives as if we were not here. These include for example, showering and getting dressed. When we shower, we often do not even feel the water on our skin, as we are often in a hurry and thinking of something else. However, contact with water is one of the most important experiences in our lives. Yet again, allow your skin to feel the water caressing it, feel the temperature, the warmth, the very essence of the water touching your skin and becoming part of your own life, of your own self through this very simple experience…

Surely there will be many other moments on your list and surely you understand the principle of how to allow yourself to be mindful on any occasion, when you would normally act automatically… Of course, it will be challenging to live a full mindful day (from start to finish.) But, if you remind yourself every now and then to use one of the moments on your list, simply to go with your senses and allow them to lead you wherever they want to take you, without fear and any expectations. This will help you become more mindful, along with the exercises suggested in this book.

Timing Mindfulness

As we have previously mentioned, this book offers you a variety of short exercises to improve your mindfulness, which should be carried out at the right time, in the right place and under the right conditions. If you are new to mindfulness, there is virtually no point in trying an exercise when you are under stress, maybe due to an important meeting at work or because you are about to take a test at school.

This is something you will be able to do at a later stage, when you are more experienced and you are better able to control yourself and your emotions. Therefore, in this chapter we will be looking at the best times during the day and/or week to do these exercises.

Even if each exercise will only last a matter of minutes, it is advisable to prepare for it. Bearing in mind that this may add some time to your exercise routine. You should always try to do the exercises when you are relaxed. Thus, relaxing before a mindful exercise is something which you need to take into consideration.

Of course, you may have your own favorite relaxation techniques, but here are some helpful hints, which may assist you:

- Take a 20 minute break from stressful activities, before starting your mindful exercise.

- Have a relaxing bath. The ideal would be to infuse your bath with a relaxing essential oil, such as lavender oil.

- Before doing your mindful exercise, take a relaxing stroll in a peaceful place or spend some quiet time in your garden or a nearby park.

- If you are used to meditating, a short session before an exercise would do wonders.

- Make sure that you are comfortable, this includes wearing comfortable clothing.

- Switch off your mobile, the television and the computer (if any of these are in the same room where you will be doing the exercise.)

- Avoid confrontational situations before doing the exercise. If you have a situation to deal with, which you know will cause you stress, be aware of the fact that it will take you time to relax before you can do the exercise.

- Hydrate! This is essential.

- Drink herbal tea, such as chamomile, or any other relaxing tea, before doing an exercise.

- Do not do the exercises after a heavy meal, as when we digest, our focus turns inward and many of the exercises will ask you to focus on what is around you and to relate to it in a balanced way.

- Do not do the exercises on an empty stomach either, as you will need energy and yet again, your focus will turn inward and onto receiving and attaining energy, this will not allow you to have a balanced exercise.

- If you like scented candles, please feel free to use them, as this will enhance relaxation.

- Avoid doing the mindful exercises when you have a lot on your mind, as you need to be flexible with the timing: if you have an issue that requires your urgent attention, rather change the timing of the exercise.

- As a rule of thumb, you should get into the habit of not dealing with problems after the last meal of the day. It is better to eat a little later and with a clear mind, than to eat with unresolved problems nagging for your attention.

- Try to set aside time to relax and enjoy life, after having your last meal and before going to sleep.

- Ensure that you are in a comfortable position when doing the exercises, as you should feel at ease with your body.

- Do the exercises in a place which is not filled with any unpleasant memories, as this may interfere with the exercise.

Looking at the average week of an average person, mindful exercises are often better done in the evenings, but this is not a rule set in stone. If you are able to set aside some time in the morning, when your mind is clear from any worries or concerns, a morning exercise can be ideal to start your day on a very positive note.

Lunch breaks can also be used for mindful exercises. This depends of course, on the length of the lunch break you are allowed to take. If you have a very short lunch break and only have enough time to eat, you may not have enough time to do the exercise.

If you find that you have fallen behind with some of the exercises, due to the lack of time or you may have purely forgotten to do an exercise, do not beat yourself up about this. As we have mentioned, these exercises can be done over a period of thirty days, but if it takes you longer, do not worry about this at all. Continue at your own pace.

Consider using your weekends for longer exercises or to catch up on the exercises which you may have missed earlier on. Most of us have much more time available and are much more relaxed on weekends, when we are not at work or at school.

There are exercises which you can try in strange "dead moments" during your normal day. These can be done at different times, these may include exercises you can carry out on the commute, while queueing, when leaving work or school etc. When doing these exercises, you will notice how much more relaxed you are in comparison to your state of mind when you experienced the exact same situations in the past.

Please feel free to repeat these exercises as many times as you wish during the day and if you feel that an exercise does not work, do not blame yourself. The likelihood is that the situation was wrong, so just try again. Do not feel obliged to follow the exact order in which the exercises are presented in this book. You should try to use and do these exercises to suit your personal and specific needs.

It would be advisable to take some time during the day to reflect on these exercises. Reflection is essential to learning and is better done when one is calm and distanced from whatever the situation may be that you are reflecting on. This will give you better insight into what you have already achieved and what you will need to do next.

If you would like to share your experiences of these exercises with your friends or family, you may do so freely. But, you need to ensure that you share this with someone who will not be judgmental and you also need to ensure that you always focus on your progress.

You are not in any way obligated to do so, but if you wish to keep a diary, this will only enhance your experience and compliment this book. Choose a dairy which has significance or holds meaning to you or design your own cover, if you wish. Furthermore, you should not try to rationalize these exercises, but express your feelings instead. Remember that it is pointless to overanalyze everything.

Maintain your focus firmly on how you are becoming a better, freer and more balanced person. It also does not matter whether you write or draw pictures in your diary, this is your personal diary, so you may do whatever you wish and hey, if you are musically talented... why not keep a "music diary" simply expressing your feelings in songs.

We have covered some of the theory of mindfulness, as well as the principles of mindfulness and in addition, we have also covered how to do these exercises in general. So, the time has come to move onto the "nitty-gritty" of this book. We will now be taking an in-depth look at the exercises which you can do to improve your mindfulness and we will cover this in greater detail, in the remainder of this book.

The Pre-Test Mindful Day

During this first week, you will have 8 days, as this first day is a bonus day! This will be a pre-test to gauge how mindful you are before starting this journey. You will repeat this during the first days of weeks 2 and 3 and after the completion of the challenge.

For the entire day, just be mindful of how you navigate the world. Pay attention to what you think, feel, and how you act and respond to situations. The goal is to be aware without any judgment or trying to change anything.

Example: When driving, be mindful of what you think about. Do you feel the urge to listen to a certain type of music or podcast? When you get to work, be mindful of the conversations you engage in and what thoughts and feelings occur as a result. Again, this is not the time to try to change anything but just take note of your own behaviors.

This Mindful Day will be like falling in and out of a dream. You will be mindful for a while and then will slip back into a non-mindful state. Once you realize you slipped back into this "dream" state, simply bring your attention back to the present. Do not get discouraged or try to change your behavior in any way, just observe.

DAY 1: Mindful Body Meditation

Preparation: Sit or lie in a comfortable position. Set a timer for 5-10 minutes. Take 5 slow, deep, calming breaths to get you into your meditative state.

Mindful Awareness

In this meditation you will be doing a body scan, focusing on the sensations of each part of your body.

Focus on: Temperature, external sensations of clothing, air, feeling hair, the pressure of body weight, and internal sensations of tightness and relaxation.

Spend anywhere from 10-30 seconds focusing on each, individual area. Once you have noted all of the sensations, move to the next body part. Start your focus on the bottom of the feet. Move up to the ankles, calves/shins, front and back of knees, front and back of thighs, hips, bottom and pelvic area, lower back and lower stomach, middle back and middle stomach, top back and chest, shoulders, neck, back of head, face, and top of the head.

Note: For this meditation, you can choose to end it once you have scanned your entire body instead of setting a timer.

DAY 2: Mindful Breathing Meditation

Preparation: Sit or lie in a comfortable position. Set a timer for 5-10 minutes. Take 5 slow, deep, calming breaths to get you into your meditative state.

Breathing Awareness

After your 5 initial calming breaths, begin to breathe normally. Focus on the feeling of the air coming into your nose (or mouth). Notice the temperature (typically it is cool). Feel the air as it travels down your airway into your lungs. Feel your chest and/or stomach rise as your lungs fill up. Notice the fall of your chest and stomach as you begin to exhale. Feel the air coming back up your passageway. Feel the sensations and temperatures as you exhale through your nose or mouth. Can you feel the air on your face? What is the temperature?

Continue this process for the remainder of the mediation. Do not try to change your breathing pattern. Simply pay attention to the sensations of the breathing. If you notice your thoughts start to wander, simply bring your attention back to your breathing.

DAY 3: Mindful Sound Meditation

Preparation: Sit or lie in a comfortable position. Set a timer for 5-10 minutes. Take 5 slow, deep, calming breaths to get you into your meditative state.

Sound Awareness

During this meditation, you will only focus your attention on the sounds you hear. Pay attention without attaching any judgment (positive or negative) to them. For example, if you hear a loud dump truck outside do not label it as loud or annoying. If you, on the other hand, hear the sound of a bird chirping, do not label this as pretty or relaxing. The point is not to pay attention to "peaceful" sounds but to pay attention to all noises without labeling them.

Start with the sounds of your breath and body. Focus only on these subtle sounds for a few moments without trying to change anything.

Next focus only on sounds you hear in the room you are sitting or lying down in. No room is completely silent. You may hear noises from your air conditioning or heat, from different appliances, or noises from any other people or pets in the house. It may be helpful to focus on one noise at a time. Focus on the noise of appliances first, then pay attention to the sound of your dog breathing, then pay attention to the sound of your kids playing, so on.

Finally, focus your attention on all the noises you hear coming from the outside. These can be animals, cars, people, or the wind. Again, it can be helpful to focus on one noise at a time. Hold your focus on each noise for a few second before scanning for another noise to listen to.

Day 4: Mindful Hand Meditation

Preparation: Sit or lie in a comfortable position. Set a timer for 5-10 minutes. Take 5 slow, deep, calming breaths to get you into your meditative state.

Hand Focus

This will be the first meditation that focuses on "being" without concentrating on different stimuli. During this, you will only focus on your hands.

Begin by paying attention to the positioning of your hands and each one of your fingers. Note the temperature of each individual finger. Focus on the weight of your hands against the surface they are lying on. If there is anything covering them or touching them, notice that sensation.

Now allow yourself to just be still. When you notice your thoughts start to drift, always bring your attention back to your hands. You do not have to focus on them the entire time, but they will help you be mindful as your mind tries to take over the mediation.

Day 5: Mindful Head Meditation

Preparation: Sit or lie in a comfortable position. Set a timer for 5-10 minutes. Take 5 slow, deep, calming breaths to get you into your meditative state.

Head Focus

For this meditation, you will focus on the sensations of your head. Typically we associate the head with a place where thoughts are constantly being fired off, but in this meditation, you will focus only on the sensations and feel what it is like to have a peaceful head space.

Feel the sensation of the top of your head. Temperature, hair follicles, etc. Move down to your forehead and repeat. Next feel your eyelids closed over your eyes. What do you see? Move down to your nose and feel your breath moving in and out. Move down to your lips. Notice if they are closed or open and if they are tense or relaxed. Finally, pay attention to any sensations of your chin. Move now to the back of your head. What sensations do you feel? Is there pressure or weight? Finally, pay attention to the inside of your head without any thoughts. Are there any sensations? Keep this mindful focus until the end of the meditation.

Day 6: Mindful Sensation Meditation

Preparation: Sit or lie in a comfortable position. Set a timer for 5-10 minutes. Take 5 slow, deep, calming breaths to get you into your meditative state.

Body Sensations

Focus on the sensations of your body as a whole. Feel its weight. Feel its temperature. Feel any sensations inside of it. Feel any sensations outside of it. Do not judge any sensation. Focus on your body being present in the moment.

When your mind starts to wander, bring your attention back to the sensations. If it helps, you can pick one part (i.e. legs) or one sensation (i.e. the feeling of clothing against skin) to bring your attention back when your thoughts start to wonder.

Day 7: Just Be Meditation

Preparation: Sit or lie in a comfortable position. Set a timer for 5-10 minutes. Take 5 slow, deep, calming breaths to get you into your meditative state.

During this mediation, do not focus your attention on anything at all. Practice sitting or lying still. When any sensations arise, try not to judge them or move.

Example, if you feel the urge to shift your body because a thought arises that said you were getting uncomfortable, let this thought pass through your head without acting on it.

When any thoughts arise let them pass through as clouds. If you get caught in a thought story, let it pass as soon as you notice, and remain still. Thoughts are nothing more than thoughts. They do not define you. They are not the truth and you do not need to act on them. You are a being who is separate from your thoughts. Sit in this state of being through the entire meditation.

Week 2

This week will focus on adding mindfulness to your daily tasks. There will be no meditation, but you are encouraged to incorporate 5-10 minutes of mindful meditation in addition to this week's activities.

Week two will be slightly more challenging than the previous week and the activities are meant as building blocks for living a more mindful life. Each day focuses on a new mindful activity. Do not feel pressure to practice the exercises from the previous day(s) during the current day, instead focus on being as mindful as possible during each new daily activity.

Day 8: Mindful Day

This is a repeat of the first day of the challenge. It is always important to periodically gauge where you are in your mindfulness journey. Pay special attention to times when you feel negative emotions or have a hard time being mindful.

For the entire day, just be mindful of how you navigate the world. Pay attention to what you think, feel, and how you act and respond to situations. The goal is to be aware without any judgment or trying to change anything.

Example: When driving, be mindful of what you think about. Do you feel the urge to listen to a certain type of music or podcast? When you get to work, be mindful of the conversations you engage in and what thoughts and feelings occur as a result.

Again, this is not the time to try to change anything but just take note of your own behaviors. This Mindful Day will be like falling in and out of a dream. You will be mindful for a while and then will slip back into a non-mindful state. Once you realize you slipped back into this "dream" state, simply bring your attention back to the present. Do not get discouraged or try to change your behavior in any way.

Day 9: Mindful Relaxing

Today, set aside some time to mindfully relax. Instead of sitting down and looking at your phone, browsing the internet, or turning on the TV, dedicate at least the first 10 minutes to sitting still. Apply what you learned during your meditations but this time in an aware, non-meditative state.

This is your time to enjoy your relaxation instead of trying to distract your mind. Feel the sensations in your body. Is anything tense or sore? Does any part feel especially relaxed? Listen to the sounds and observe the sights. Any thoughts that come to your mind, let them peacefully float out. Remind yourself that this time is for relaxing and anything that you need to think about or handle can be done at a later time. Practice this every time you plan to "take a break" and relax today.

If you have an opportunity to go outside, enjoy all the sights and sounds of nature. If you have time to watch your children play, savor every moment without allowing yourself to become preoccupied with something else. You will find that this type of relaxation calms your mind rather than distracting it.

Day 10: Mindful Conversations

Anytime you have a conversation with someone today, be mindful throughout the entire experience. Listen to everything being said without thinking how you are going to respond. Also, be mindful when you are talking. If anything said elicits a feeling, note it and be mindful of what thoughts prompted that feeling. Do not, however, allow this to take away from you being mindful during the conversation. Just note the experience and you can reflect on it after the conversation has finished.

For example, if talking to a co-worker about your boss provokes feelings of anger, make a note of it and do your best to bring your awareness back to the present conversation instead of focusing on your thoughts. After the conversation, think about what exactly was said and the thoughts that came up that caused the anger. (Note: Tomorrow there will be more discussion and time to practice this technique).

If others are having a conversation but you are not an active participant at the moment, listen without placing any judgments or thoughts on what you hear. Allow the words others are saying to enter and exit your awareness without holding on to any piece you heard.

Day 11: Mindfully Combat Negativity

Today you are going to be the observer of your emotions as if you are a doctor studying a patient. It may be beneficial to keep a thought journal to track your emotions and thoughts.

Pay attention to any time you have a negative emotion, such as anger, resentment, sadness, frustration, annoyance, anxiety, depressive feelings, guilt, etc. As soon as you notice the emotion, be mindful of what you are thinking. Outside factors never cause negative feelings. It is the thought attached to the situation that causes the feelings. Understanding what thoughts you are attaching to situations will help you understand where your negativity comes from and also help reduce it. Often we have a negative feeling and then attach more thoughts to support the negative feeling which in turn increases its intensity. By simply taking a step back, and being mindful of your thoughts and the situation, you are able to stop this process before it gets out of control.

When you have trouble getting out of a negative mindset, focus on being mindful in the current situation. Use techniques from meditation to help with this. Think of it as riding your bike down a steep hill. The top of the hill is the environment, then a negative thought comes along and gives you a little push down the hill. This hill can be very small or it can be gigantic. If you allow your mind and emotions to take over, you continue to pick up momentum and before you realize, you are speeding down a hill, out of control, with no way of stopping yourself. Now, if you insert mindfulness immediately after that push, the ground begins to level and you realize it was just a small hill and you quickly regain control.

Today, focus on being mindful as soon as you feel any negativity. Take the situation for what it is, pay attention to your thoughts, and you will notice this can quickly begin to lessen your negative emotions. Bring your focus to the present moment (sights, sounds, etc.). This will help stop you from rolling down that hill of negativity.

Day 12: Mindful Walking

If you are able, schedule a mindful walk for yourself today. Make sure the walk is at least 10-15 minutes and try to be mindful the entire time. If you are unable to schedule this walk, make sure anytime you walk today you are mindful. This can be a walk from your car to a building, a walk from the couch to the refrigerator, or a walk to the next cubical at your office. It does not matter how long or short, just make it mindful.

Check in with your body: How does it feel when you are walking? What can you hear and see during this time? What does it feel like for your feet every time you take a step? As always, do not allow any thoughts that creep in to stay. Do not judge, good or bad, anything you experience. If your feet hurt from a long day, focus on just the sensation and do not label it as pain. If you take your dog for a walk and he begins to pull, do not label him as a bad dog for doing so. If you see someone wearing a nice watch, do not think you like the watch. Objectively observe. It is just a sensation in your feet, your dog is pulling and you feel sensations in your hand as you restrain him, and it is not a nice watch, it is just a watch.

If you find you fall back into old habits and place judgments on anything, never dwell on it.

Dwelling only comes from placing judgments on yourself. It comes from thinking about past events, so always remind yourself to stay in the present. That moment has already passed and every moment is a time to refocus on your mindfulness.

Day 13: Mindful Commute

Anytime you travel or commute today, plan to be mindful. This could be your commute to and from work, it can be driving the kids to school, it can be running errands or going to the gym. It also does not have to be when you are driving. If you bike or walk to places, be mindful during those activities. If you take public transportation, also remember to be mindful.

During any of these commutes, practice all of the sensation-focusing exercises you used during your meditation practices. Do not listen to any music, news, or podcasts. Just let your mind become aware of all the sensations you are feeling, hearing, seeing, and smelling.

If commute with other people, be mindful of all conversations during this time. Listen to everything being said without thinking how you are going to respond to it. If others are having a conversation, listen but without placing any judgments or thoughts on what you are hearing. Allow the words others are saying to enter and exit your awareness without holding on to anything.

If you struggle with anger while driving or comminuting, this is the perfect time to implement the mindful techniques discussed during Day 4 (Mindfully

Combatting Negativity). Read through those instructions again to help remind you of the techniques.

Day 14: Mindful Meals

Be mindful anytime you eat today. Do not engage in activities that distract your mind, such as watching TV, texting, or surfing the internet. If you are around others and engaging in conversation, make sure you remain mindful of the eating process.

With every bite of food, taste the flavors, feel the textures and temperatures, and hear the sounds. Feel the food traveling to your stomach as you swallow it. Do the same any time you take a drink. Pay attention to how your body feels as you eat or any thoughts that may pop into your head.

When do you notice you are getting full and have had enough nourishment to stop eating? You will likely find it takes you longer to eat this way and some people eat less as they notice they get full much earlier than usual.

Week Three

Since you have accomplished so much this far, you have built up some strengths and have more courage when it comes to situations that you tend to avoid or are triggers for your anxiety. Since you have weeded out some of the unnecessary items on your lists, it is easier to focus on your other problems left for you to deal with. This week, every day you should focus on:

- Read your extended awesome list 2-3 times a day.
- Record your anxiety levels and progress.
- Write out hypothetical worries.
- Journal what you are grateful for.

Day Fifteen

Choose another weekly goal for yourself that pertains to a problem that contributes to your anxiety. If you miraculously have none left, kudos to you! Regardless, find something that you would like to improve in your life. Draw out the tasks to accomplish your weekly goal and take on one of those tasks today.

Go for a walk around your neighborhood or at a new location to give you a change of scenery. Walk for at least 8 blocks. If you pass other people on your walk, smile at them and ask them how they are doing. If they don't respond, shrug it off as nothing personal.

Relax later by meditating for 30 minutes. If you must think during this time, only envision positive occurrences in your life. Imagine yourself overcoming all your struggles and having the freedom to accomplish whatever you do without anxiety dictating your happiness in life.

Day Sixteen

Make it your goal today to confront a hypothetical worry. For instance, if you assume the worst case scenario like your card getting declined even though you know you have money in your account, perhaps try to create that scenario. Not that you are necessarily supposed to go to a store or smoothie shop and try to buy something that you can't buy, but if you feel like taking the challenge, by all means, go for it as long as you aren't shoplifting. Try to create a hypothetical situation and formulate what the most likely outcome could be. For instance, if you can't pay for something when you get to the register, you can't pay for it. They won't prosecute you. Heck, sometimes they will give you your item for free if it's food, just to be kind people. There are plenty of other scenarios that you can create that fit your hypothetical worries.

Pick three songs today to either dance or sing to. If you dance, dance your heart out. If you sing, sing your heart out. Hopefully, your neighbors will hear you. After that, find a humorous film to watch before you head to bed.

Day Seventeen

Take another hypothetical worry and find some way to address it. These types of worries can be various so you might have to get creative, just like with yesterday's goal. In attempt to keep a positive mood, try doing the pen exercise again. This time, instead of 5 minutes, try going for 7 minutes. Do some yoga sometime throughout the day for 30 minutes and then find time to relax by reading at least 30 pages of your favorite book.

Day Eighteen

Today, your goal is to approach an attractive person. It doesn't matter if you are married or in a committed relationship. Attraction is a real thing and being human means you are going to get your nerves worked up when you approach someone that is attractive. You don't have to tell your partner about this activity. It won't give you an appearance on the"cheaters" show. The point is to actively get you outside of your mind. Anyways, approach this person and either drop a comment on something or find some way to start a conversation. The worst thing that can happen is that they think you're weird, which shouldn't matter too much to you if you are in a relationship. If you are single, think of it as the fact that the person was not really a match made in Heaven. He or she was a project for you to complete in order to work on yourself.

For exercise, do 30 jumping jacks today along with some stretches. Find time to relax better by listening to relaxing music while taking a hot bath with an essential oil of your choice.

Day Nineteen

Take time to organize any or all of your household items that could use it. As mentioned, cleaning and organizing de-clutters the brain. This statement is even more so for organization. If you don't have too much time to dedicate to organizing, spend at least 30 minutes in one area or more. Go for another walk this week to get some exercise and try to go for at least 10 blocks this time.

Once you get back home, sit outside for 10-15 minutes and enjoy the outdoors. Don't distract yourself with media devices. Simply focus on the nature around you and relax for a bit.

Day Twenty

Today, either go to a zoo or a museum. You must go by yourself and you must see everything that is there. This will help you be comfortable with yourself in situations where you are surrounded by other people and families. You may even find it a bit more relaxing and enjoyable to do an activity like this by yourself. Once you get home, do some meditation followed by a hot bath with aromatherapy.

Day Twenty-One

You have finished your third week of challenges! Awesome! Give yourself a break today from all that you had accomplished this week. Get yourself out of the house today and treat yourself. Write down a list of all your accomplishments from this week and add them to your awesome list. By now, you may have realized how much you have accomplished and that will only motivate you to accomplish even more.

Week Four

You have now made it to your last challenge week. Pretty exciting stuff huh? By now you should feel somewhat invincible. This week will focus on the most aggressive goals so far in order to pump you up and keep you going.

Here is a list of things to remember to do every day:

- Read your further extended awesome list 2-3 times a day.
- Record anxiety levels and progress.
- Write out your triggers and assumed triggers.
- Write out what you are grateful for.

Day Twenty-Two

Find your weekly goal for today and do what you have always done and make a game plan of tasks to do in order to complete it. Accomplish one of those tasks today. After that, go to a store and buy a hula hoop. Go home and hula hoop for 15 minutes continuously. Afterward, relax by taking a hot bath with either Epsom salts or aromatherapy.

Day Twenty-Three

As you are writing out what you believe to be your assumed triggers and actual triggers this week, pick an assumed trigger to confront today. Make a plan as for how to confront it and go. Refer to breathing exercises and positive mental exercises if you get overwhelmed. Whether you were successful or not, go home and do some simple stretches. Relax afterward by calling up a friend to talk to either about your progress or your unsuccessful attempt. They could offer some helpful insight to give you a better shot of success if they happen to understand you well.

Day Twenty-Four

Today, instead of picking an assumed trigger, pick a trigger that you are absolutely sure of. Make your game plan, and go. Just go straight through your anxiety and that will be the only way to overcome it. Remember to refer to the breathing exercises and positive mental exercises. After your attempt, go home and dance to 5 fun songs giving yourself one minute breaks in between songs. Afterward, find a funny movie or videos on the internet that will make you laugh.

Day Twenty-Five

Today, find a movie showing at a theater that you would most likely enjoy and go see it alone. You may feel awkward being by yourself when there are couples on dates or groups of friends and family, but this activity will only help you learn to be okay with yourself and only yourself. Sometime today, try to go swimming or do yoga for at least 30 minutes. Help yourself unwind by sitting outside for 30 minutes also.

Day Twenty-Six

Just like yesterday, do an activity alone. Go shopping alone. Even if your funds won't support it, go to at least 5 stores and look at their items. While you are shopping, try walking around the whole entire mall. Depending on how big or small your mall may be, this is where you get your exercise for the day. When you get home, unwind from the overstimulation you may have felt at the mall by listening to relaxing music for 30 minutes.

Day Twenty-Seven

Today, look at your list of triggers and pick another one to confront. If you were unsuccessful with the last trigger that you tried to confront, attempt to confront the same one once again. For exercise, do 40 jumping jacks to get your blood pumping. You might want to try this exercise after your daily goal in order for it to be used to blow off some steam. Afterward, take 30 minutes to meditate with or without relaxing music.

Day Twenty-Eight

After all the triggers you confronted this week, take this day to take a break and choose whatever type of exercise and relaxation technique you would like to do. You have made it this far and that is enough accomplishment as it is. Try going shopping again and buying at least one item you might have had your eye on but were unable to purchase the other day.

Day Twenty-Nine

As your thirty-day, challenge starts to come to an end, think about one more big goal that you would like to accomplish for yourself. Make another game plan and take charge of when you take steps to your own tasks. To get your dose of exercise today, find a nice park to take a walk in. Take a hot bath when you get home to relax and unwind.

Day Thirty

Congratulations! If you have gotten to the end of the challenge! This means you have supreme success even when your anxiety convinced you things would go otherwise. Before you part from your challenge, sit down and really write out what all you have accomplished this past week, and all the many more things you'd like to continue accomplishing. You must feel pretty pumped after all of those activities to get you out of a boring routine and into one that requires you to step out of your mental box and take note of your life. By now you will have learned much more about yourself than you did, to begin with. You might even have some exercises and relaxation techniques that you have learned work best for you and that you actually enjoy. By this point, all of these activities should easily become habits in your daily life if you keep at it. The worst part is over now. The rest is just deciding what you want to do from here on out.

What Exactly is Inner Peace?

People refer to inner peace in different ways. Some believe that it is a special feeling one attains when one becomes wealthy. However, wealth has nothing to do with inner peace, if it did, then the wealthy would have contentment and wouldn't become too greedy in seeking more and more wealth.

Experts believe that the best definition of inner peace is "self-acceptance". It is simply the act of letting go of your worries and accepting yourself for who you are. Some experts believe that inner peace can best be described as a state of being mentally and spiritually at peace within your body, mind, and soul, and with sufficient knowledge to keep yourself in this state for the rest of your life.

From a spiritual perspective, it seems there is a common agreement on the route to inner peace and that is "self-acceptance". This means the only way you can achieve inner peace is by accepting the things you cannot change about yourself and embracing the ones you can change with courage and commitment.

Peace of mind is often referred to as absolute serenity or calmness. Being at peace with yourself also means you are completely healthy and you are not stressed nor anxious about anything. Inner peace of mind is also associated with complete bliss, contentment, and happiness. When you have inner peace, you are definitely in another state of enlightenment or consciousness; however, this state can only be achieved through conscious training of your mind. This training can come in the form of prayer, meditation, and some exercises such as Yoga and Tai Chi which target both your conscious and subconscious mind.

Most spiritual practices attached to inner peace focus on knowing more about yourself (self-awareness). Finding inner peace has been associated with connecting yourself to higher levels of existence.

The main reason we find it extremely difficult to achieve inner peace is that we allow distractions, challenges, and obligations to overwhelm our conscious and subconscious minds. When your mind is influenced by too many distractions, your thinking will not follow a rational path, but you will continue to base your actions on what influences you, especially the feelings you have.

Most people have difficulty embracing their inner peace. You don't have to turn to religion to find inner peace. To many, finding peace and happiness within the little joys of life can be extremely challenging. Through a step-by-step process explained in this book, you will discover how pleasurable it can be to learning how to find inner peace.

The world today has become a confused place where selfish interests, greed, and personal ambitions have forced many people to abandon common sense in pursuit of personal gratification. Social media recommendations and endorsements have encouraged many to live helplessly without peace of mind, but with some simple techniques, you will be able to harbor constructive criticisms in your heart and learn to do away with one-way criticisms that may force you to abide by some people's ways of life.

"Nobody can hurt me without my permission" – Mahatma Gandhi

According to the words of Mahatma Gandhi, the first step towards achieving inner peace is to determine that you will not allow anyone to hurt you deliberately for no reason.

You know you have achieved an inner peace when you experience the following:

- You stop comparing yourself to others. The act of comparing yourself with others will always undermine your self-worth, and you will be distracted from your personal goals and objectives.

- You start living your dreams, not because of what you want to prove or through the act of impressing people, but because it is what you decide to do. You achieve inner peace when people's opinions of your personal preferences don't matter.

- The moment you realize that you are the primary enemy of your own inner peace. It is what you accept into your mind that stays and your subconscious mind is always influenced by your conscious mind.

- The moment you believe that you can achieve anything you want to, though you still realize that it will take some time, the right attitude, and the right passion.

- The moment you realize that no single person can give you complete happiness except yourself.

- The moment you realize that love is not about winning or losing, but is something that should be nurtured and grown.

- The moment you realize that being ignorant of your own strengths and weaknesses will not make you achieve inner peace.

How Chaotic Lifestyles Ruin Your Inner Peace and Happiness

The present world is a fast-paced one and it is increasingly more difficult for many people to remain at peace with themselves. Your inner peace is often subjected to quite a number of enemies. These enemies come from the social lifestyles and personal habits we develop over time. There are three major lifestyle habits that can ruin your inner peace and happiness, these are:

- Regrets over your past mistakes
- Anxiety over the problems you will face in the future
- Ingratitude for the blessings you have already achieved (dissatisfaction)

Other reasons why you are unable to achieve an inner peace include:

- Resistance
- Doubt
- Living in the future
- Ego

- Ignorance of your strength and weaknesses
- Perfectionism
- Defeatism
- Materialism
- Dualism
- Escapism

Regrets over past mistakes

Your past regrets are the prominent reason why you cannot achieve inner peace. You need to understand one thing, regrets will never change what has happened and until you make amends and let go off your past, you will never prepare yourself enough for the present. Hanging onto your past is a distraction that will disable you from being 100% present in the process of deciding your next action; the fear of the past repeating itself is crippling to honest forward thinking. When your past shows up, you feel guilt for the mistakes you've made and even things you didn't do, and your actions will definitely be guided by your desire to alleviate such guilt. You need to remember that no action or reaction will be enough to absolve you from your past guilt and you will never achieve inner peace if you still feel that you should be punished for your sins over and over again. Feeling guilty for your mistakes forces you to get stuck to your past, and you want to develop an attitude to alleviate the pains of guilt- this will definitely prevent you from achieving inner peace.

Ingratitude for the blessings you have achieved right now

Dissatisfaction is one of the problems that forces mankind into greed. This is a state of continuous striving that always blinds us to the blessings we have and the ones we are capable of having. We want to get more, and do more, and in the quest of getting more, we get into trouble. Between our quests to get more, we may start having momentary satisfaction and happiness, but sooner or later we enter the struggling and striving modes once again.

Anxiety over the problems you will face in the future

Living in the future is an outright waste of precious time, and it is similar to wallowing in your past because no matter what you do, you cannot rewrite what has happened. Neither can you dictate what the future holds. Worrying too much about what will happen in the future will only make you develop turmoil within yourself; it will consume your entire mind, making you to feel uneasy about yourself.

You need to realize that your present thoughts determine where you are right now. You may continue to think that the right partner will come along when you have money, or that you will be completely happy when you are healthy. You need to divert your energy and thoughts to the present moment if you want to be happy because no one knows the future.

Defeatism

Defeatism brings fear into your mind every time, and fear itself is the biggest source of pain and struggle because it runs so deep into your mind. Fear can be primitive in nature and when it takes hold of your subconscious mind, it becomes the hardest feeling you can fight. Fear prevents you from achieving happiness in many ways; you are afraid of losing someone you love, you may be afraid of disapproval, you may be afraid of missing out on opportunities, or you may be afraid of not being good enough.

Fear is strong, but we often end up making it stronger and so much worse. The moment you harbor fear, you want to develop resistance and push it away and thus you may end up compounding the pain.

Resistance

Developing resistance is one of the reactive ways we tend to deal with challenges; it makes us want to hit life in the face to take revenge. Instead of critically looking at a situation and dealing with it in a mature way, we tend to react negatively and this adds to our inner conflict. Resistance to challenges can manifest in several ways. Some of these include procrastination, denial, and avoidance. Continuously arguing with people over non-serious issues and the feeling of being overwhelmed are some of the symptoms of resistance.

Doubt

Doubt can simply be defined as an absence of faith or trust. When you don't have absolute faith in your own capabilities then you definitely won't be at peace with yourself. You may often find yourself questioning every move you make, thus, you don't have enough motivation to deal with any situation. Doubt will always reduce your sense of self-worth by feeding your mind with fear and fueling your resistance to all situations.

Ego

Your ego is that part of you that puts a veil on your inner peace. When you are too full of yourself, you believe you don't need help from anyone. One thing your ego does is to remind you of your state of separateness and why you need to prove that you are better and stronger than everyone else. Your ego remains one of the sources of sadness in your life; it creates a conflict of interest against others.

When you have inner peace you will remain in harmony with everyone; it gives you a sense of unity and you will start feeling the sense of connection between you and your environment as well as every other person. Though it may be difficult to get rid of your ego, you can subdue it for the sake of achieving inner peace. You need to focus on your higher and better self instead of focusing on satisfying your ego. Your ego will always place numerous demands on you every day , and when you allow it to influence you, you eventually lose your inner peace and happiness.

Ignorance of your strength and weaknesses

There is an aspect of each and every one of us that is invisible but quite real, and this is the spiritual higher-self. Your spirit being is the person you really are. You may continue feeling unfulfilled until you start nurturing that aspect of your life that is invisible. Your spiritual being should be regarded as a strength, thus, when used in an appropriate way it tends to give you the extra push you need to achieve your goals and objectives in life. When you learn to nurture the divine part of yourself, you will listen less to the expectations of the world and concentrate more on your own purpose.

Materialism

Materialism is the idea that you must have everything (material possessions). The quest to have it all will force you to do anything to get what you want, perhaps even stealing and killing. When you have a new gadget or device for instance, you will definitely be pushed to buy the one that will be released the following year because you don't want your friends to make jest of you for being "old fashioned".

Dualism

Dualism is a kind of life that is pulling one in two different directions, and it will keep your mind tangled in knots. You may want to keep up with the status symbols you have achieved and at the same time you want to live beyond your means. Most of the celebrities we adore today are living dual lives, they are actually bankrupt but keep portraying an image of self-sufficiency.

Perfectionism

When you are a perfectionist, you don't want to leave any room for mistakes. The problem with being a perfectionist is that you will never achieve an inner peace because you cannot handle criticism, therefore, you want everything to be perfectly done always. Being a perfectionist will not help you learn new things and grow, therefore, you need to work on attaining maturity rather than perfectionism.

Defeatism

Defeatism can also be referred to as pessimism. You are always afraid that something will eventually go wrong and as such you don't put forth your best effort to achieving your aims and objectives. Defeatism will make you under-perform, thus you end up achieving much less than you actually could have.

Escapism

When you are afraid of failure or being corrected, you want to escape from the situation. There is no way we can run away from our problems, whether they are caused by you or someone else. You need to keep in mind that you are the only one who can subdue your personal struggles, no matter how daunting they may seem.

Positive Characteristic Features of Mindfulness

The fast pace of life of the present world has forced many to be less mindful, but when the positive features of being mindful are considered one will definitely want to learn the act of being mindful. Life is all about making choices and each choice you make will eventually affect the quality of the life you live. Mindfulness can best be described as a mind-body medicinal practice. You don't have to empty your brain and become religious in order to be mindful, it is all about simple techniques practiced every day. Here are some of the characteristic features of a mindful person:

- They focus on the present moment only

When you are always lost in thoughts about your past and the future, it is hard to focus on what is happening right before you. When you focus on what is happening right now, you will be opened up to the positive things unfolding right now. You will also be open to things that might unfold in the future as you wouldn't won't have negative preconceived ideas of how your future should turn out because you want to make the best out of the present.

- They are always fully present

Are you spaciously conscious of what you are feeling in the present moment? You need to understand that you can have a brighter future when you take care of the things you hear, feel, see and do right now!

- They are always open to new experiences

Rather than shutting down their feelings and experiences because of their inabilities to handle them, individuals who are open minded are willing to learn and experience new things. They don't hold onto old and ineffective beliefs. Instead, they are open to thoughts and feelings that may naturally arise because they know such feelings are mere momentary sensations and they can change at any time. Individuals who are mindful of new thoughts believe that new experiences will evolve over time and they will provide a lasting solution to their problems.

- They are non-judgmental

Being mindful means you are slow to judge and condemn yourself or others for who they are or what they believe in. Being mindful means you do not categorize your thoughts as bad or good until you are compelled to act on them. You need to understand that all feelings serve a purpose, whether to protect you or incite you to take instant action that will bring about positive result. When you are mindful, you accept situations consciously and not irrationally. Being mindful also means you must be willing to extend a non-judgmental attitude to others as well.

- Accept things and situations as they are

When you are mindful you accept different situations more easily. When you are mindful, you don't force your own vision and beliefs into reality, likewise, you don't feel like you are a victim of circumstances, and don't bemoan challenges as unfairness that life throws at you. Rather, you see reality the way it is and tolerate what you can before your vision eventually fits into current realities. Mindful people are always capable of handling different situations that come their way because they have learned to use reasoning and common sense approaches.

- They are connected to people and their environment

Individuals who are mindful are rarely involved in strife and fights with other people. They reflect peace wherever they go and don't react sharply to what people say or think about them. When you are connected to your experiences, you no longer feel needy like people who are not mindful of themselves or their situation.

- They have non-attachment to other people's misdeeds

Mindful people don't hold onto negative deeds and experiences because they are aware of the fact that life is a continuous flow. People have a strong attachment to the past deeds of others when they are fearful or when they are needy; however, mindful people have the confidence that they can adapt to any situation.

- They are optimistic

Mindful people believe that when the door to an opportunity closes, another one will open. They are compassionate with others and they always have peace radiating in them.

- They are compassionate

Mindful people are kind towards others; they love people for who they are and are ready to help them when in need.

The First Phase of Becoming Mindful

(10 Practical Approaches to Being Mindful)

When you begin to introduce the act of mindfulness into your life by deliberately subjecting your mind and subconscious mind to deliberate positive thoughts through simple meditation practices, then you will begin to witness a positive transformation in your life. Developing an observing mind can be performed in several ways but it starts with simple steps such as watching your daily experiences, including what you feel inside and around you, and then carefully noticing your automatic response before redirecting your attention to your present moment.

When you are aware of the enemies of your inner peace, then you will start learning how to make conscious efforts to get rid of them. you need to overcome your struggles from within and watch as your world begins to turn around positively.

Before you go deeper into the acts of mindfulness, there are some practices you should start with in order to complete the process of being mindful with ease. Here are the first 10 procedures to follow:

#1 Embrace your enemies mentally (acknowledging your present situation).

Acknowledging your present situations and the emotions that accompany them is the first step towards being mindful and achieving internal peace of mind. Make sure you welcome your present situation of unmindful behavior into your conscious awareness and listen to what those beliefs have to tell you.

#2 Lookout for the trade off

There must be something that is forcing you back to experiencing the pains of your unmindful attitude. You need to learn from the thing that subjects you to pain and reduce your powers of rejecting them. Your beliefs and emotions should protect you rather than inflict pain on you, but when the perceived threat is just imaginary, you continue to subject yourself to undue sorrow. What you get from repeated feelings may be growth opportunities; therefore, you must identify the imaginary cause of your unhappiness.

#3 Feel the pains as much as possible

Whenever you notice the feeling of struggle, pause for a moment and pay attention to such feelings as they course through you. Make sure you follow the physical reactions you are experiencing, and feel the pain and stress as much as possible. You will notice that the more you immerse yourself in the pain the less you struggle with it. You need to understand that feelings are always like waves, very strong at the beginning, and then subsiding over a period of time.

#4 Simplify your routine

Most times we exercise resistance against unpleasant situations of the past we do so because of too many commitments, but when we learn to clear some clutter from within and without we start experiencing more inner peace. Learn to break up your schedule into simpler units.

#5 Practice more contentment

You can never become mindful and achieve inner happiness when you are not grateful for what you have presently. The joy you need is around you. All you have to do is to pause for a moment and look at life with openness and curiosity and you will achieve the transformation that you have always wished for. The struggles you are experiencing now are as a result of the habitual behavior, emotions, and beliefs you have harbored in your heart for a very long time. The more you release these beliefs from your mind, the lighter your heart becomes. Appreciate the little things and moments you have now!

#6 Learn to prioritize peace over performance

Learn to put any task or deed that brings more joy and happiness to your mind ahead of those that force you to measure your performance. When you are always measuring performance, you may never achieve inner peace because you want to perform better always, and that will eventually stress you out. With inner peace you will be motivated to perform much better, but without the stress and anxiety, you will be prone to fewer errors.

#7 Learn to accept the inevitable and unchangeable

One of the best possible ways to achieving inner happiness and a state of mindfulness is to accept yourself for who you are. That does not mean you must stick with old bad habits, it simply means you must accept what you have little or no power over, and learn to cope with them. Don't worry about your looks, height, weight, and other physical attributes. Rather you should learn to wear what suits you and do what makes you feel good. Learn to keep friends that make you feel good.

#8 Practice the act of assertiveness

Just like any other habit you must learn, in the first phase of becoming mindful you need to practice the act of being assertive. With assertion, you gradually become disciplined. You have the right to your own opinions just as anyone else does. Being assertive does not mean you put your needs ahead of the needs of others, if you do then you are aggressive. Assertiveness means you aim for a "win-win" situation for an amicable resolution.

#9 See your temporary failures as learning curves

Learn to resist guilt because it steals your inner peace any time it shows up. Guilt is a toxic emotion that will motivate you wrongly; therefore, you must challenge the reasons for your guilt. You need to note that everyone fails at one time or the other, but you must embrace the concept of having a healthy attitude towards each failure because it makes you open to learning from it. Always learn to challenge those "should haves" and "musts", and replace them with "could haves"; this will help you live your life on your own terms.

#10 Practice self-affirmations everyday

One perfect way to encourage yourself to achieve inner peace of mind is to practice positive self-affirmations. You can write these affirmations down and read them out loud in front of a mirror on daily basis. One positive affirmation you should remind yourself of is, "No matter what comes my way, I will surely find a way to get through". Self-affirmations must be practiced at any given chance, whether you are on break, during your quiet times, when exercising or when you are simply walking in a park. Self-affirmations have a positive effect on your mind and body and it is the perfect way to start achieving inner peace.

The Second Phase of Becoming Mindful

(10 Practical Steps to Become Mindful)

The second phase of becoming mindful introduces you to the practical steps that will make your mindfulness practices even stronger. The secret to the success of mindfulness practices at this stage is consistency. You need to practice the steps frequently in order to achieve the best possible results.

#11: Practice mindful breathing techniques

Mindful breathing practices help you take control of your emotions when those feelings of past guilt arise. You can practice these exercises while standing or sitting, and it is ideal to find somewhere quiet and suitable. All you need to do is remain still and stay focused on controlling your breathing during the exercise.

Start the process by breathing in and out slowly (this is one cycle, and should last for about 6 seconds). Make sure you breathe in through your nose and then breathe out through your mouth, and let your breath flow in and out effortlessly. Take a break and then let go of your thoughts for about a minute; these include the things you want to do later in the day or abandoned projects you need to get back to, and then remain still for another 60 seconds.

Try and purposely watch your breathing pattern and focus your senses along the pathways through which your breath enters your body while filling you with life and energy, then gently watch as the air works its way up through and out of your mouth, with its energy dissipating. With the air flowing out of your body you start feeling some relief from the guilt of pain and pressure you have been experiencing for a while. With this technique you will be able to introduce yourself into the act of meditation. If you enjoy practicing this 3 minutes of calming exercise, why not repeat it two or three times to achieve an even better result?

#12 Practice Mindful Observation

Once you have mastered the act of mindful breathing, your next step is to practice mindful observation techniques. This exercise is quite simple, but remains powerful in helping you achieve inner peace. This practice is designed to reconnect you to the beauty of your environment. This is something you always miss out on when you rush to work early in the morning.

To practice this exercise, simply choose a natural object from your immediate environment and focus on watching it for about 3 minutes. The best objects to consider using for this practice are insects, plants, the moon or clouds. During this exercise make sure you focus on nothing else except the object you are observing, and relax yourself into harmonious concentration. Concentrate on the object as if you are looking at it for the first time and watch its every movement and detail. Make sure you allow your mind to be consumed by the object's flow of energy and its role in the natural world. This practice will gradually return your power of concentration and your ability to live in the moment without worrying about your past and the future- eventually it helps restore your flow of happiness.

#13 Practice mindful awareness

Mindful awareness practices are designed to help you cultivate the habit of heightened awareness and the appreciation of daily tasks and the results you achieve from such tasks.

To perform this exercise simply think about something that happens more than once every day, most especially a thing you often take for granted (for instance, opening the door), and at the very moment you have your hand on the door knob to open the door, simply pause for a moment and remain mindful of where you are, how you feel in that moment, and where the door will lead you. Similarly, consider how you learned to operate a computer, and appreciate how you are able to comprehend the ways to use the computer.

Each time you have a negative thought, this exercise will help you pause and then label the thought as negative and unhelpful, thus you can eliminate it quickly before it goes deeper into your thoughts. When you are thankful for the little things such as the food you prepare and share with family and friends, you will definitely learn to understand the dangers of harboring negative thoughts in your mind.

#14 Practice mindful listening

Now that you are already learning the act of observing and being aware, your next activity is to practice mindful listening habits. This exercise is designed to open your ears and mind to different sounds and in a non-judgmental way. You need to remember that both your conscious and subconscious mind are affected positively or negatively by what you see and hear on daily basis, but when you practice the act of listening mindfully, you will develop a neutral and present awareness that allows you to listen to sound without any prejudgment or preconception.

To practice this step of mindfulness, simply select a song that you have never listened to before; this may be a song from your own collections or you can simply turn on the radio and listen to something new. Close your eyes and put on your headphones. Make sure you resist judging the music by its genre when it begins playing. Instead, you should allow your mind and body to be immersed in the journey for the duration of the sound. Allow your mind and body to explore every aspect of the track. Just let go of your possible dislike for the music while allowing your full awareness the permission to dance along to the tune. The idea of this exercise is just to listen and become entwined in the composition of the music while relieving yourself of any misconception of the genre. If you hate rap music for instance, you should try out a rap song for this exercise.

#15 Practice mindful immersion

The purpose of mindful immersion is to cultivate the habit of contentment in yourself. Without contentment you cannot achieve a lasting inner peace. With this practice you will be able to escape from your persistent striving that you are caught up with on daily basis. Rather than waiting anxiously to finish your everyday routine in order for you to move onto something else, you will learn to perform your regular routine without placing too much stress on your body.

An example of mindful immersion is when you clean your house. Try as much as possible to pay careful attention to each component of the activity. Rather than continuing with this regular activity, why not create an entirely new experience from it by noticing every aspect of your actions and reactions? For instance, feel the motion when vacuuming the floor, and feel the intensity of the muscles you use when washing the dishes and then you can determine a much more effective way of handling those chores. One of the ideas of mindful immersion is to become more creative and then discover new experiences within familiar routine and tasks.

With mindful immersion, you wouldn't have to labor constantly and think about finishing tasks, but you are now becoming aware of every step and have begun to fully immerse yourself in each small progress made, therefore, you will be able to take each activity beyond the regular routine by aligning yourself emotionally and physically to it. When you master the act of mindful awareness, you will enjoy each activity.

#16 Practice the act of mindful appreciation

This is the practice of recognizing things that you do every day that go unnoticed or unappreciated. To perform this exercise, simply pick 5 things or people and with the aid of a notepad, write these 5 objects or people down.

The purpose of practicing this mindfulness step is to give thanks and appreciate the things you may have thought were insignificant in your life. These should be things or people that support your existence but are rarely appreciated. Most times we do not appreciate certain things or people because we get carried away by the desires to achieve bigger things. When you learn to appreciate the clothes that provide warmth for your body, the flowers that make you smile in the morning, the parents that send you money in school, and the nose that helps you smell the fresh air, you will eventually become mindful of everything that matters to you.

THE FINAL PHASE OF BECOMING MINDFUL (5 PRACTICAL WAYS TO TAKE CONTROL OF YOUR MIND AND ACHIEVE INNER PEACE)

The final phase of mindfulness practices involves the use of powerful mind-changing techniques such as visualization, meditation, self-affirmation, hypnosis, and healthy hygiene practices.

#17 Practice the act of mindful visualization

Simply put, visualization is the process of creating positive images in your mind. Visualization has been proven to be effective in teaching humans how to be mindful because the images we create and relay on a daily basis determine what influences our decisions on daily basis. The main purpose of visualization is to create mind power by forcing the images of what you want into your subconscious mind. Visualization relies on mental rehearsal, and it brings those things you are not aware of into your consciousness.

With visualization techniques you will live and feel as if it is happening to you right now, and with continued practice, you will eventually get rid of negative thoughts from your mind. Visualization builds your self-esteem, and you don't have to live within the guilt of your past. To practice visualization techniques, picture yourself having that dream job you always wished for and in your office giving instructions to your subordinates, then remind yourself of the steps you need to take to get to that position and start actively taking those steps.

The more you have the image and thoughts of positivity in your mind, the more you start witnessing a positive transformation from within your subconscious mind because all those negative thoughts have now been replaced by positive ones. This is the point where your inner peace and happiness returns.

#18 Practice self-affirmation techniques

Just like visualization techniques, self-affirmations also work perfectly to boost your self-esteem, help you become mindful of your situation, and makes you achieve your inner happiness. Your affirmations must be positive statements. You need to stop asking yourself negative questions such as, "what will happen if I fail this job interview?" The main motive behind affirmations is to attract what you want - for instance, always bring to memory those positive things you achieved through your strengths. Stop making use of negative affirmations such as "I am too weak today" or "I am so nervous". Always keep in mind that making a mistake is not the end of the world, therefore, you should say positive things to yourself like, "I am getting the job today" and "I have a great idea I will implement this year".

Remember, positive affirmations are always in present and future tenses; they must not include past tenses. Always make your affirmations short and simple so that they become easier for you to remember.

#19 Practice guided meditation

Guided meditation is one of the oldest and traditional ways of bringing back your wandering mind. It helps you retain focus and also boost your memory. Meditation is quite supernatural because it heals your mind and soul while emphasizing your psychological strength. Guided meditation can be performed while standing, sitting, or in any position that is convenient for you.

To practice guided meditation, balance your body on a flat surface (you can spread a mat on the floor before sitting on it), then make sure you pay attention to your shoulders, ribcage, belly, and your chest. Don't force yourself to control your breathing, rather just focus your attention. If your mind is wandering while meditating, simply shift your focus back to your breathing, and then maintain your meditation practice for about 5 minutes. Stop and practice it once again.

When meditating, focus on solving one simple problem at a time, then you can focus on resolving bigger issues as you progress in your meditation.

#20 Practice healthy hygiene

Feeling good and happy starts from how you treat yourself on daily basis. If you have not been taking care of your body in a while this is the time you need to do so. Having inner peace has to do with how you look on your outside and inside and you can definitely enhance your attitude by enhancing your body.

Make sure you floss your teeth at least twice a week and brush your teeth twice a day. Make sure you wear clean clothes and put on a good-smelling fragrance. Make sure you tidy up your home and let people know that your life is being transformed positively. You should try low-impact exercises that are pleasurable, for instance, swimming, cycling and the use of a treadmill can help you tone your muscles and look fitter. The more results you achieve from these exercises the happier you become, and you will definitely want to achieve more.

Ways of Sustaining Your Mindfulness in the Midst of Negativities

Now that you know what it takes to be mindful and happy you should do whatever it takes to retain your new habits and inner tranquility. Here are the things you need to do to ensure that you sustain your mindful habit:

#1 Keep practicing the act of mindfulness until it becomes part of your natural routine.

Now that you are aware of the simple techniques that can help you become more mindful and happy, you need to make such techniques more relevant to your everyday life by applying them to everything you do. Within a short period of time they will start influence your actions.

#2 Be realistic with being mindful

You must be aware that negative people will always be there to influence your behavior, but the more you make them realize that you will not trade your happiness for their interests, the more they will start respecting you. Do not impose bogus demands on yourself because you want to be happy.

#3 Don't be too hard on yourself

You need to set a target for yourself for a specific time you wish to regain your positive mindset; however, you must not force yourself through the process of regaining your mindfulness. Let things work out naturally and they will eventually become part of your lifestyle.

#4 Give room for errors and challenges

Becoming mindful is not something you can achieve in a single day. You need to keep practicing it. Sometimes it can be difficult to forget about certain experiences, but the good news is that you can change your subconscious mind to accept what you want, therefore, you need to keep doing what you are doing to achieve the best result.

#5 Develop the attitude of loving yourself and the people around you

You cannot become mindful and achieve inner peace and happiness if you don't learn to live at peace with everyone. When you learn to embrace your future without fear and remain optimistic, you will naturally be attracted to people that will eventually help you achieve your dreams. You need to learn how your mind works, and then you can focus your attention on controlling it in such a way that it does not wander away from those things that give you happiness and peace of mind.

#6 Reward yourself

There is no problem rewarding yourself when you make headway with your new lifestyle as regards achieving inner peace. Rewarding yourself for new achievements will serve as a motivation and remind you of the importance of being mindful and achieving an inner peace. Inner peace helps you achieve more positive things that you wouldn't achieve ordinarily, because negative thought will never allow you to move forward.

#7 Become friends with yourself

As you begin to learn more about yourself through mindfulness, it is ideal that you approach your new lifestyle in a friendly manner and not with criticism. When you learn to embrace difficult feelings, you will learn to love yourself, and when you love yourself, you will radiate love to the people around you.

#8 Always practice your guided meditation

Everyone who practices meditation discover something new, and for this reason, it is important to continue guided meditation to direct you to a new path.

#9 Find a community of people who practice mindfulness activities

You will always find a community of people who share the same passion as you for achieving inner peace through mindful acts. You need to seek out and join in such a community and learn from them. Through the inspirational stories of others you will find motivation for achieving your own dreams.

#10 Always commit yourself

Don't just say, "I will practice these steps on some days", but make sure you are committed to the practices highlighted in this book to achieve the best possible result.

Conclusion

Although anxiety is no easy fix, there is a way to overcome it. By taking a look at the big picture of your life and how it fits into everyone else's lives, this helps your perspective become a bit more appropriate. By learning that this is a mind over matter issue, even if it is also physical, you allow your mind to become the key to overcoming your struggles. Practice words of affirmation and verbally declare that you will be successful. When worst comes to worse, learn to laugh at the ironic nature life can give us. Find ways to challenge your hypothetical worries and laugh at them when you see the ridiculous picture they paint in your mind. Remember that everything passes with time, just like any attacks. Know that the only way that you will overcome anxiety itself is by facing it. Don't ever go around it, just go through it.

When you observe the choices and lifestyle you make for yourself, you may realize that you are picking your own poison and that alternatives may be a necessary choice when it comes to eliminating opportunities for anxiety to exist. By choosing a healthier lifestyle, you are also choosing a healthier state of mind. Stop yourself when your thoughts tend to wander.

By learning the physical and mental exercises, you have also learned how to take charge of what happens mentally and physically in your body when anxiety is present. Although you may feel nervously out of control, you have a better concept of what you do have control over. Anxiety will never have a cure, but you will always have a choice. By stripping away the bodily sensation of fear that anxiety presents you, you can allow the nervous energy to excite you as an alternative and push yourself to do new and challenging things.

Perhaps, if you were too afraid to attempt some of the steps that were outlined, remember to cut yourself some slack and remember that anxiety is still physical and can be more so in other individuals. When stated that it is a mind over matter issue, it might not be the same story for everyone. Anxiety is still a condition and some individuals need extra assistance when coping and fighting against it. Talk to your doctor about your struggles and he or she may give you something to help physically bring down levels of anxiety so that you can have more mental control over your struggles. If that is the case, challenges yourself to re-attempt the steps outlined in this book. It will only further empower you and help you start a successful cycle of accomplishments in attempt to battle your negative and anxious cycle that you are tired of living with.

Book 3: Minimalist

Your 30 day mental rework guide to a minimalist life, to declutter your home, mind and emotions

By

Beatrice Anahata

Chapter 1: Minimalism

True minimalism is quite different from what you see in mainstream media. Many people are leading "minimalist" lifestyles to the extreme, eliminating everything they have from the picture and living with next to nothing. In reality, this is often a delusional depiction of what minimalism truly is. These scenarios are often attention-grabbing for their shock value, and lead people to believe that a minimalist lifestyle means that you live a life of lack and struggle. After all, how joyful can you be when you have nothing to fulfill your day-to-day needs?

If you want to be a true minimalist, you must first understand exactly what minimalism is, and what it isn't. To make it very simple: minimalism means to lead a life whereby you only use what you need for regular basis. Anything and everything else that no longer serves you or brings you joy is either thrown away or given away, thus freeing up space in your physical environment, as well as in your psychological one. To understand this description on a deeper level, we will further explore the concept of minimalism.

What Is True Minimalism?

Being a true minimalist means that you lead a life where you no longer hold on to things that no longer serve you. When you look around your home, you no longer see clutter because everything has a purpose and is used on a regular basis. Anything that no longer has a purpose is eliminated from your life, either by way of trash, donation, or sales. You no longer spend your life collecting and hoarding "treasures" in your home. Instead you live free from the consumerism lifestyle. Your life isn't spent acquiring more stuff; it is spent enjoying life and doing what you want when you want, free of any physical burdens. You release emotional attachments to objects, and you find peace in life itself, instead of in objects that prove to be obsolete over time.

How Do You Benefit?

There are many major benefits that arise from living life as a minimalist. First off, when you eliminate unnecessary clutter from your home, it has a highly therapeutic action on your mind. Right now, look around the room and notice five different items that you would consider to be clutter. Take a moment and truly think about what these objects mean to you. Do they bring you joy or happiness anymore? Or do you hold onto them for some tie to the past that they resemble for you? Or, do you simply hold onto them because you are too proud or too lazy to let them go, so you just do nothing instead? The clutter we store in our houses never comes without consequence. We often feel guilty about these items. We may have buyer's remorse or guilt that we no longer live under the circumstances that we once did when the item came into our home. We may have resentment towards the item for always becoming a source of clutter and stress, instead of simply disappearing and no longer being present to cause this stress. We wish that the item would disappear because the burden of actually having to get rid of it means that we would have to face emotions we don't want to face: guilt, despair, and other difficult emotions. When we get rid of these items, though, we eliminate these emotions altogether.

Aside from the emotional and psychological benefits of removing clutter from our lives, there are other benefits as well. For example, when you have fewer belongings, it becomes easier to maintain them. You no longer spend your entire life cleaning up clutter, because clutter ceases to exist in your life. Everything you own has a purpose, and it has its spot to be stored so that it never gets in the way. It makes life significantly easier. As well, you no longer have to spend your entire life working tirelessly to purchase new stuff and maintain existing stuff. You don't have expenses related to fixing broken objects or acquiring new ones, so you simply have to make enough to afford to live your day-to-day life. You are free to do whatever you want with your spare time, without fear of leaving behind a house full of objects that serve no purpose other than to tie you down and fill your life with stress and misery. You can travel, move, and do virtually anything you desire to do without any attachments to the belongings you own. Case, the thirty-day journey toward adopting a clutter-free minimalist lifestyle starts with the single most crucial step of deciding to carry out the most definitive lifestyle makeover ever.

To many, a minimalist lifestyle denotes a harking back to the times of our cavemen ancestors with little or no access to all the modern amenities that make life worth living. However, the ones who understand the real implications of a minimalist lifestyle realize that its basic premise is that you have a surfeit of what you need to lead a happy and fulfilling life and by thoughtlessly hankering after what you don't have and don't need, you invite needless anxiety and unhappiness.

Before you even begin to take any concrete steps toward adopting a minimalist lifestyle you should hold a clear understanding of what it is not. It does not necessarily mean turning your back on every semblance of the modern way of life. You can lead a clutter-free life without having to make any seemingly appalling sacrifices.

However, you do need to radically change your mindset to the extent that you start valuing yourself above the material things, the acquiring of which you had hitherto made the raison d'etre of your existence. You can do that by dwelling on the benefits of leading a clutter-free minimalist life-

1. Decluttering sets you free

Once you start getting rid of the substantial number of material possessions that you have been cramming into various parts of your home, you will feel a lot lighter and freer. For one there will be more space in your home, allowing you greater freedom, both in terms of being able to move around more easily and no longer having to take care of so much stuff.

The sense of liberty will not just be a physical one, but also a mental one, in that you will be free of the baggage of the past, enabling you to focus on what matters to you now. To take an extreme example, if you still hoard the toys you played with as a child, wouldn't you feel a lot better, if you gave those away to someone's children who might need them? You are hardly likely to be using those toys again!

2. Helps you find focus

Having too many possessions dulls your focus. For one, all the property needs to be taken care of, and in many cases where you have bought stuff on credit, there is the added stress of having to pay for it. Isn't it far better to get rid of the bills in one fell swoop and instead focus on the more important things in life like building relationships? Rather than pay the monthly installment toward the fancy sports car, you could perhaps use the money for your children's education.

3. Save money for the important things of life

Rather than splurging on a possession that adds no real value to your life, living a life with less expenditure you could do two things at the same time. One reduces your dependence upon money, and two, get rid of debt the bane of American society.

Imagine a life where you spend as much as it takes to get by and not spend most of your living hours trying to make enough to finance your profligate lifestyle. What is the point of that?

4. You live better

A minimalist lifestyle makes very little demands on your time, and the sense of freedom and lightness that it provides you makes you healthier.

Consequently, you get to live a contented life, precisely the way you want to be.

For instance, you may be living a minimalist life with the minimum of possessions, a relatively small workload and plenty of time to spend with your family. The thing about this lifestyle is that it is a choice based one. You can make your life as minimalist as you like. There is no duress involved.

The important thing is that with all the physical and mental clutter gone from your life, you will enjoy better health and have more energy to live your life to the fullest. It is precisely for this reason that minimalism is growing in popularity by the day. More and more people realize that this way of living is the best. It lets you live life the way that it is meant to be in the most simple yet amazingly effective way. It shows you a whole new paradigm of going about your daily existence-the right one.

Get Down to Business

Adopting a minimalist lifestyle is definitely a leap of faith, but if you have decided that it makes sense for you to have one, nothing is to be gained by dilly-dallying or postponing the inevitable. However, you can do this is a manner that makes you feel comfortable, as the whole idea behind leading a minimalist life is to eliminate stress and not create it.

What you can do to feel better about the entire process is to do it in tandem with others who are inclined to adopt the minimalist and clutter-free way of life. It could be close or even distant members of your family, friends, and colleagues. You could get together and start a thirty-day contest about who gets rid of most clutter on a day to day basis for a period of thirty days, at the end of which you can decide a winner on the basis of who is most successful in getting rid of most stuff.

The game could easily be made more interesting by making the rate of getting rid of unwanted possessions a progressive one. For instance, the first day you could start with one item, the second day with two things, the third day with three items and so on till the thirtieth day when each one of you will have to get rid of a whopping thirty items!

As you can imagine the game might be quite easy initially, but will soon become increasingly difficult to play. Think of what all you can get rid of, clothes, furniture, decoration pieces, electronic equipment, kitchenware, old books, footwear, bottles, cans and so much more. You could donate, sell or throw away the extra stuff lying at home, but the idea is to keep to the schedule.

As you progress through the days, you will realize how much unnecessary stuff you had been holding on and how with each disposal you somehow feel a little lighter and freer. There will be those among you who will be very loath to let go of some of the stuff but will eventually see the wisdom in removing past deadwood. Some of you will not be able to bear the sense of loss or separation and may drop out of the contest, way before it reaches a conclusion.

By the time you reach the end of thirty days, you will likely have not only got used to living with far less possessions than before, but actually seen that it wasn't as difficult as you had imagined that it would be. Not only that you would have begun to experience the benefits of leading a minimalist life. If any of your fellow contestants too make it, you will feel elated in their company and if they haven't, you can thank them for giving it their best shot and helping you in your journey toward a new more fulfilling lifestyle. For all you know they might reconsider their decision to leave the field and return to the fold someday.

Decluttering of your life, of course, comprises of much more than getting rid of some odd possessions. It has much more to get rid of the whole paradigm of the avaricious- materialistic-perennial-growth driven approach to life. An approach that would have you forever chase the chimera of worldly success without allowing you to pause to reflect upon what you actually want from life.

Thirty Days to Prepare

A minimalist lifestyle is not only about getting rid of material possessions. It has to do far more with mentally letting go of your attachment to a thoroughly materialistic lifestyle. You will most likely find it harder to manage the latter rather than the former, especially in the first thirty days of your attempted makeover. That is why you will have to undergo this process a day at a time. Given below is a thirty-day plan of action that lets you both test the waters and ease into a clutter-free minimalist lifestyle

1. Don't Go Online- We have started living our lives more in the virtual world than the real world thanks to the technology revolution. If possible, this has made our lives even more disconnected with what is truly important for us. The very term virtual reality is a giveaway in that it is not real. How can anything that is not real, provide us with lasting happiness?

Try going completely offline for a day and get a sense of a different kind of freedom, where you are not bombarded with information about the goings on in the far corners of the materialistic world. Neither do you feel the pressure to keep up with your hundreds possibly thousands of Facebook friends who should not really mean a thing to you?

Instead, you could try meeting up with your real friends who you know would always stand by you. Focus on enjoying the meal that you are eating, rather than snapping it with your smartphone and posting a picture to be liked on social media!

2. Reduce your digital dependence- Now that you have a fair idea about the advantages of spending more of your time in the real world than in the digital one go ahead and reduce your dependence upon the latter. One realizes that you may not be immediately able to get off the grid, but you can sure restrict your access to it.

You can do this by checking your emails, texts, and social media messages just once in a day. Simultaneously stop posting on social media, if not deactivate the accounts. Don't keep multiple devices that keep you hooked to the Internet. Instead of making most of your purchases online, start visiting stores. This will not only let you see and feel, what you are buying, but also interact and connect with the sales people. Getting out of the pernicious digital ivory tower will do your body and soul a world of good.

3. Take up meditation- For you to get away from the attractions of a consumerist and materialistic world, you need to be able to connect with your own innermost thoughts and feelings and find out what it is that you actually want. A profound way of doing that is by taking up meditation.

It has repeatedly been stated, and scientifically proven that meditation has immense physical and mental health benefits. By calming you down, it stops the flow of a whole lot of extraneous and adverse thoughts passing through your mind and lets you have a rare clarity about what really matters to you. This will help you understand how a minimalist lifestyle firmly puts you on the permanent path to peace, tranquility and real progress.

4. Give up cribbing- We have all been fed on a constant diet for striving for more than we have and indeed need. What this does is programs us to crib and be dissatisfied with what we have. How sick is that?

We have to stop cribbing ceaselessly and be grateful for the great gift of life and cherish every moment of it. Ending the need to crib is not always as easy as it might appear, as we are so used to demanding more and more and more. Once you snap out of this habit, you will begin to realize, how truly blessed you are already and instead of cribbing you will learn to savor what you have.

5. Take to reading- Reading has taken a backseat in today's times what with myriad entertainment options available online. Nothing exemplifies a minimalist lifestyle better than reading. There is nothing ostentatious about reading, yet there is a wealth of knowledge to be acquired here.

Spend time learning the wisdom of the world by reading instead of splurging your wealth on gadgets and gizmos which you will probably not use half the time. Reading, on the other hand, is inexpensive but can keep you absorbed for hours.Though it's possible that you might not be able to keep up with the Joneses by indulging in this activity, but then you will need to for you would have found yourself.

6. Prioritize- Take an entire day to figure out what you want to truly achieve in life. Is it the unmindful pursuit of one material goal after the other or is it doing the best for your family by providing ensuring that they lead a happy, content and healthy life?

You have got to choose between ceaseless hankering after materialistic goals which add no value to your life or choose a lifestyle that enables you to live your life at a deeper level. Do you want to be beset with lifestyle diseases or would you rather live a simple and robust life?

7. Make the right commitments- The commitments you make in life determine how much you are in tune with a minimalist lifestyle. If you are committed to attending a party every weekend, you can forget about adopting it. On the other hand, if reducing the carbon footprint weighs upon your mind, you are on the right track, in so far as adopting a minimalist lifestyle is concerned.

8. Make a fresh start in the mornings- Even though a minimalist lifestyle is all about uncomplicating your life, it does require for you to introduce a modicum of discipline to your life. Starting your mornings with an invigorating ritual like a brisk walk, yoga or going for a run would help you focus your thoughts and channelize your energy in a positive and fruitful direction.

9. Eating Sensibly- Somebody has rightly said that we are what we eat and a minimalist lifestyle would have you eat simple and sensible meals. You wouldn't be expected to gorge on lifestyle disease inducing processed food, high in sugar and fat content.

Simple, nutritious food like whole grains, fresh fruits and vegetables and fish will keep you both healthy and fit. Besides, you will not end up spending a fortune on them

10. Learn to enjoy solitude- Nobody knows you better than you yourself. Spend time with yourself in solitude, and you will discover that it takes very little for you to be happy.

11. Stop Wasting- Our modern consumerist lifestyle generates an appalling amount of waste- discarded food, empty bottles, clothes that we buy and never wear, electronic junk and so on and so forth. You have to begin opting out and the time is now.

12. Use public transport- That fact that most of us go about in our personal vehicles might be very convenient for us but puts inordinate strain on the planet's scarce natural resources. Besides, it makes us lazy and fat.

Start using public transport instead. It will both reduce your carbon footprint and make you fitter in that you will have to walk to the bus or subway station.

13. Shop sensibly- There are so many enticing clothes, jewelry, accessories, cosmetics, electronic gadgets and a wealth of other objects of desire that tie us to a world of excess. Break free by shopping sensibly only for what you really need.

14. Plan ahead- Living a minimalist life is something that you have to commit to long term. You need to plan ahead for the entire year so that you know what exactly you are getting into and what it is that you are required to give up. Besides, you will have to learn to live your life in ways that are very different from before.

15. Learn to not buy- Minimalist living is all about your having to buy as little as possible. Most of our needs are easily met, and we have to get out of the habit of buying something or the other every day. Stop yourself from buying anything in the next twenty-four hours to prepare yourself for a whole new way of living.

16. Don't multitask- Get out of the bad habit of multitasking. Far from achieving more, you end up losing focus on everything you take up simultaneously. Instead, learn to be absorbed with one task at a time and do it with all sincerity.

17. Start keeping a gratitude journal- There is so much to be thankful for in life, and one best practice to accomplish that is to start keeping a gratitude journal. Start noting down instances for which you should express gratitude, and you will realize how happy you are.

18. Stop indulging in one-man-up ship- Life is not about showing others that you are the boss. This may get you temporary gains in the corporate world, but make you deeply unhappy inside. Give up this bad habit and be good to others, so that they are good to you.

19. Work on identifying and removing stress triggers- All of us have stress triggers which keep us from being happy all the time. The minimalist lifestyle encourages you to understand your stress triggers and work toward eliminating them.

20. Spend a day that is entirely unplanned- While discipline and following a set daily schedule makes sense, there can be a day set aside that is completely unplanned. This is in acknowledgment of the fact that we are not machines or robots, but human beings with free will. See how the day unfolds in the most unexpectedly interesting ways.

21. Give up a goal - We have made our lives so miserable in pursuit of so many goals. Try giving up a goal and see how liberating that can be. If you can't into a dress size that you easily did twenty years ago, accept that fact and put on something that suits you instead.

22. Analyze your last five purchases- We are so used to cluttering our lives with useless stuff that we pick up almost on a daily basis that we do not even realize, how this phenomenon has trapped us in this never-ending phenomenon of buying for the sake of buying. Analyze your purchases of the last five days, and you will be astounded at how much of it was unnecessary.

23. Reclaim your sleep- In our quest for success we are willing to sacrifice so much, even a good night's sleep. Once we realize that the journey we were following was an unwise one, we can focus on better ones. Like following a daily routine that exercises our body and relaxes our mind enough to make us fall asleep without much trouble.

24. Lend a helping hand to someone- We need to take a break from the cut-throat world of our workplace where self-interest dominated everything else. Medical science tells us, this is bad for our health. Try to help someone every day. It will bringer and stronger and brighter feeling as you go along.

25. Reconnect with nature- We are the children of nature and get rejuvenated in its bosom. Get out of your artificial cocooned existence more often. Start with a day-long trip to a lakeside or a riverfront. Recharge your batteries by becoming a part of nature once again and not its adversary.

26. Learn to share- Our natural resources are scarce. Learn to share them. Become part of a carpool and share your daily ride to office and back with someone.

27. Become more social- Keep your smartphone at home and try engaging people in conversations at public places-at the shopping mall, airport, and restaurant. Reconnect with real people.

28. Stop using disposable products- Stop your dependence upon disposable things. Water bottles, food packaging, plastic cups, disposable tissue and so much more which is rendering our planet toxic.

29. Reuse and reuse- Instead of using and throwing things, start using and reusing them. Don't drink water from a paper cup, use a proper glass instead. Buyer fewer clothes and wash them more often. You can start making these changes to your lifestyle so as to be able to seamlessly adopt a minimalist way of life.

30. Give up automation- Most of the gadgets that we use at home are actually adding nothing to our lives and only making us lazy, fat and unwell. Try to stop using your washing machine, microwave oven, dishwasher and vacuum cleaner and do the cleaning and washing manually. It might be challenging work, but you will be fitter and healthier for it.

Do You Have to Get Rid of Everything?

Being a minimalist doesn't mean you are getting rid of everything you have. Instead, it means that you are getting rid of everything that no longer serves you. If you love painting, for example, by all means, keep your painting supplies. But if you don't love painting and you simply keep the supplies around "just in case you'll use them one day," then it is time to get rid of them. If you were going to use them, you would have by now. And, if you decide to pick up a paint brush in the future, you can simply purchase new supplies or even attend a painting class instead of acquiring all of the supplies and soon just have them stored.

Anything that actively serves a purpose in your life can and should be kept. However, anything that is only kept out of obligation or fear of not having it when you need it should be eliminated. The truth is, we can easily acquire new things when we find we need them in our lives. There is no sense carrying around a large selection of items that we no longer need, especially when we are not using them. That is when your belongings become clutter, and your clutter becomes stressful, and your life becomes miserable. If you want to make a change, you have to learn to eliminate what no longer serves you and keep what does.

Can You Ever Shop Again?

Of course, you can! Minimalism doesn't mean that you will never shop or make purchases again. It simply means that you must learn to be more mindful about what you are bringing into your house. If you are purchasing objects that you know you will not use for longer than a few days or weeks, then it is likely a better idea to overlook that object completely. Worst case scenario, see if you can rent one or borrow to a friend to see if you actually like the object. If not, then simply don't invest your money, time or space into acquiring the object. Instead, move on!

Where Is the Joy in All of This?

The greatest sense of joy that you will acquire from the minimalist lifestyle is the freedom. You no longer have to work twice as hard to acquire things and maintain them. Instead, you can reduce the amount of effort you put into things by purchasing less clutter and storing less clutter. You save a large amount of time this way, and you provide yourself with the opportunity to do virtually anything you desire. Instead of being stuck in the consumerism cycle, you can begin to enjoy life itself genuinely. You can start experiencing life as it is, free of any physical thing that holds you down. You will no longer feel obligated to invest so much time in maintaining and protecting your belongings, and it will be easier for you to pack things up and move along. You can move, travel, and do virtually anything you want without fear of being held back by your physical items. As well, you will have more free time due to not having to work as hard to have what you have.

Minimalism is not quite like what they tell you it is in mainstream media. It isn't about living in an extreme state of lack, where you have virtually nothing in your life. There is no rule that says you can only own a set number of items or only certain things can be kept if you are going to be a true minimalist. You can own any number of things and be a true minimalist. The key is making sure that all of those items are valuable, and that you will use them for an ongoing period. As long as the intention behind your belongings is proper, then you can consider yourself a true minimalist.

Remember, the journey is about bringing joy and freedom. The process of eliminating your belongings and freeing up your physical space and your psychological and emotional space is not about creating a new and different situation that brings stress and discomfort. It is about relieving stress and discomfort altogether and learning to live life in a way that is more fulfilling and satisfying to you. It is about bringing freedom, happiness, and joy together in your life by no longer being trapped in the consumerism cycle, and learning to live a life that is no longer bound by physical belongings that don't even serve you. When you learn to live life like a true minimalist, then you will be able to enjoy all of the many values that life has to offer, the true minimalist way. If you are ready to start living life like this, then you are ready to commence day one of your 30-day minimalist challenge.

Chapter 2: Days 1 to 10

The first ten days of minimalism are going to be some of the hardest. In this time, you are going to start eliminating things from your life and learning to live in a whole new way. You may feel a variety of emotions at this time; the experience will be unique to you. If you must, take your time and do it slowly. The purpose of this challenge is to successfully teach you to practice minimalism with a comfortable transformation, not to shock you into a new lifestyle that will leave you with regret and misery over the choices you have made. Practice each day as it is provided and you will realize how simple the transition can be and how rewarding liberation from a physical tie can be, as well.

Day 1

The very first day of your challenge is going to start out simple. You want to collect a box which you will keep in a central location in your house. Then, you will place one item in there that you wish to donate. For the next thirty days, you will continue to place one single item into this box. This is an easy task that will allow you to eliminate thirty items from your home that you no longer need.

By doing it just one at a time, you make it extremely simple for you to let go of these items, as you have a full 24 hours to process the idea that these items will be gone for good. There are two challenges in this act: first, you are not to remove anything from the donation bin. Once it's in there, it must stay there. Second, you must only work one at a time. The idea is not to get overwhelmed or shocked by jumping into a new lifestyle. It can be hard to see your entire home change rapidly, even if you have wished for it to happen for a long time. If you move too quickly, you may regret your actions and end up purchasing several items to replace what you no longer have within' your home. The goal is to learn how to live without these items, one at a time.

As a bonus task for day one, you might want to take a journal you already have lying around your home, or take to the notepad on your computer and start writing d your experience as you work through this process. Writing out how you are feeling each day will help you process the changes you are making. Then, when you potentially reach a point of struggle, you can return to your writing and read why you made the changes you did. Be sure to share how you felt before you started the challenge and the intimate reasons as to why you started the challenge in the first place. This will help set you up for success if you ever find you reach a point where it is becoming difficult for you.

Once you have done this, you have completed your day 1 activities for the 30-day challenge.

Day 2

"Out of sight, out of mind" is a phrase we know all too well in life. When we collect clutter, we often shove it aside into places where we can no longer see it so that we don't have to regularly revisit the guilt and regret we feel around investing our time and money into these items. When we do this, however, we do not face the problem head on. Instead, we sweep it under the rug and pretend there is no problem, to begin with.

For day two, you are going to sort through your junk drawer, or junk drawers if you have many. You are going to get rid of everything that turns these drawers into junk, and you are going to reclaim them for a new and fulfilling purpose. This will allow you to clean out the depths of your home, which will feel like you are cleaning out your deepest, darkest secrets. It is also a wonderful activity for the second day of your challenge because the change is in the deeper parts of your home - somewhere where you won't see it immediately, but you will know it is there. Think of it as a chance of physically rewiring the subconscious of your home.

To do this activity, take everything out of your drawers and completely clean them out. Before you do anything else, decide what new purpose these drawers will serve. Then, you can begin sorting through everything. Eliminate anything that is not useful or does not bring you joy. Then, anything that fits the specific purpose of the drawer can be neatly replaced back inside. If you wish to enhance the organization process, you can include drawer inserts. However, there is no need for these if you do not desire them. Only purchase them if they will genuinely make you feel happier and keep your belongings more organized.

Once you are done going through everything, eliminate anything that you no longer need or want. Typically, junk drawers are filled with smaller treasures that have little to no value or purpose. Unless you have something valuable that is worth selling, simply throw the rest in the trash. In most instances, there is nothing worth donating in these drawers. It is all simply garbage that we are too attached to throw out.

Once you have finished emptying your junk drawers and repurposing them, you are done with day two. Feel free to write about the experience and how it made you feel. Remember, everything you write d can help you process emotions greater than simply thinking them. You will also give yourself something to refer back to, should the transition become emotionally difficult at any point in the future.

Day 3

Today you are going to go a little deeper into your experience. You are going to trash everything that you no longer need. Any items that are broken beyond repair, or that have been sitting around collecting dust while you hope to make use of them in the future should be trashed today. Too often we carry around items from place to place because we fear that without them we will not have access to the benefit that they once offered. Do not allow this fear to keep you from trashing items that no longer belong in your home, or any home.

As you are doing this, take your time. Go into each room, and only trash what you can immediately recognize as trash. Look at your belongings with unbiased eyes and genuinely ask yourself what needs to be eliminated. There is no need to leaf through the depths at this point, as you will go deeper in the coming days. Right now, you simply want to remove the trash from the surface of your home: all of the areas that you can see when you initially walk into the room.

Eliminating the trash first makes everything easier. The process of getting rid of things that you have been holding on to out of fear, guilt, or other unhappy emotions can be extremely liberating. Often, when we are too guilty to get rid of something, we also feel unwanted feelings any time we look at it. For example, perhaps you purchased an accessory for your living room and then later decided you no longer wanted it, or it broke, and you told yourself you would fix it. You might keep it around or store it in your closet because you feel guilty that you invested your money in it. Money is a resemblance of time, so what you feel guilty about is that you invested a significant amount of your time into acquiring that object and then it broke or became useless to you. Now, you don't want to throw it away because you fear that it will resemble lost time, and that makes you feel sad or perhaps angry. Instead, you keep it. Every time you look at it now you will feel guilt, anger, sadness, and perhaps many more unwanted or negative emotions. When this happens, you have now invested time into making money to acquire an object that you don't want, and then you invest time into feeling bad over not wanting it anymore. Some people invest days, weeks, months, and even years feeling this type of guilt over a variety of their belongings. By throwing these items away and being done with them once and for all, you liberate yourself from those negative emotions.

Remember, you don't have to comb through the depths of every room and throw everything away. At least, not yet. In the coming days, you will experience several opportunities to throw stuff away that you no longer want or need. Before you're done day three, remember that you are still supposed to be putting one item into your donation box. Then, if you desire to, you can write about your experience and what you felt when you were eliminating these unwanted and unneeded items from your home and your life.

Day 4

Almost everyone has a guest room, or something similar, where they begin storing items that they aren't using. These items are often things that we never use but don't want to eliminate either. They may hold memories from your past or hopes you had for your future. You may have used an item once or twice and then placed it in the guest room, truly believing that you would use it again at some point but you never did. It is the time that you eliminate these items from your guest room or storage room, and let them go from your life.

This is something that you will want to take a few hours on, to give yourself enough time to tackle the entire task truly. Make sure that you do it all in one day, and that you don't leave any of it for later. Often when we are organizing, we promise ourselves that we will do more later and then we simply shut the door and "forget" to finish our project. You do not want to do that with this room. This room is one of the most toxic rooms in our homes if we are not careful, and you must be sure to complete it all in one day. You might want to take breaks throughout the process, but don't quit until the entire project has been completed.

To complete this task, start in one corner of the room. There is no need to try and do it all in one go. You can take your time and focus on one thing at a time. Start with one box, then another. Work your way around the room slowly. Have designated areas for garbage, donation items, items you want to sell, and items you want to keep. Once everything has been gone through, you can organize the items you want to keep back into respective storage spaces. The rest should be dealt with that day. Throw your unwanted items away, put the donation bin in the car so you can take them to the donation drop off, and post any items you want to sell. Give yourself a timeline for items that you are selling: if they do not sell in seven days, they get put in the donation bin where you are still accumulating your one item per day for the remainder of this challenge.

Once you have completely cleaned out your guest room, take some time to freshen it up. Vacuum, turn out the bed, open the blinds, and wash the windows. Give the room a little life to bring it back from the consumerism tomb that it previously became. When you are done, go ahead and do your daily journaling so you can write about how it felt to work through these items and face the reality of who you were, who you are, and who you genuinely want to become.

Day 5

We often carry things around in our dressers that we no longer want or need. Today, you are going to donate some items that you no longer need to a charity or organization who can then give them to those in need. This task should be fairly simple. Head into your wardrobe with a plastic shopping bag and walk out with the bag full of items you no longer want or need. Let those who need the items have them, and you can find joy in knowing that your wardrobe is now much lighter and easier to manage without as many clothes in it.

Eliminating things that you no longer wear can feel great. It helps you identify who you are, and who you aren't. When we hold onto clothes that we no longer fit into or that we simply don't wear, we become honest with ourselves about who we are. Often, the root cause for us holding on to these items is that they represent who we think we are or who we want to be, and they allow us to secretly wish for who we aren't. This creates a series of negative side effects including several that can be damaging on self-esteem and self-confidence. The best thing to do is to eliminate these items and maintain the clothes you do want and wear on a regular basis.

While you are at it, if you find any clothes that are ripped, excessively worn, or stained, you can throw them away. These items are no longer useful and keeping them around simply to fulfill your physical attachment to your memories is not beneficial to your wellness.

Once you have completely gone through your wardrobe and filled your bag with donation items, put the items in your larger donation bin to be taken to the donation drop off at the end of the challenge. Also, put your daily item in the box. Then, you can do your daily journaling. This will mark the completion of day 5 of your 30-day challenge.

Day 6

Today you are going to focus on loose paper in your home. The primary things you will focus on include: newspapers and magazines, mail, and receipts.

Newspapers and magazines tend to build up in our homes. Often, we don't even read them anymore because we can find all of that information online. It is time for you to take appropriate action with your newspapers and magazines. Today, you are going to recycle everything that you have not read and will not read. Then, you are going to contact all of the places that deliver you newspapers and magazines, and you are going to request to end your subscriptions. Unless, of course, you actually read any of them. If you do find yourself actively reading them as they come in, it makes perfect sense to continue receiving them. Simply vow that once you're done, you will throw the remainders into the recycling so that you do not have them piling up around your home.

Mail seems like such an archaic form of communication these days, yet we still seem to receive so much of it. Today, let's take some time to think about how you handle mail when you get it. Do you throw away the junk mail, or do you let it sit on your counter until it has piled up? Do you shred confidential mail, or do you keep it in a pile and say "I'll do it later"? What are your habits around the mail you receive? Today you are going to go through any piles of mail you have sitting around and deal with them. Unwanted junk mail will be put in the recycling, and unnecessary confidential mail will be shredded. If there is an option, such as with bank statements, you should go online and opt for online communications instead of paper communications. Then, you are going to put in place a new strategy for when you receive mail from this day forward. Whenever you receive junk mail, it should go directly into the recycling. Whenever you receive confidential mail that does not need action, you will shred it immediately and put it in the recycling as well. Anything that is confidential and requires action should be placed in an accessible spot, acted upon as soon as possible, and then shredded and eliminated.

When it comes to receipts, it is important that you stop piling them up around you. If you keep receipts for tax purposes, be sure to have an effective filing system in place and as soon as you come home immediately file your receipts from the day. Any receipts that are not necessary should be immediately discarded. If a cashier asks if you need a receipt and you do not require it for tax purposes, you should request that they simply recycle the receipt for you. This will keep you from having to remember to do it yourself later on.

Paper can overwhelm your home, car, and if you have one, your purse as well. We often accumulate so many pieces of paper that do not have direct importance in our lives and all it creates is a massive amount of clutter. For the paper that is important, we rarely have strictly enforced rules for ourselves for how we will deal with this paper. Today, you are going to change that.

Once you are done dealing with your paper, you can put your one item away in the donation box. Then, you can complete your daily journaling activity. After that, you are completely done for day six of your 30-day minimalist challenge!

Day 7

Earlier this week you donated an entire bag of clothing items. Today, you are going to actually organize your dresser. When you are doing this, you want to make sure that you are making everything accessible in a way that makes it easy to keep your dresser clean. You will also get a second opportunity to get rid of anything you no longer want to keep.

The first step to organizing your dresser is to remove absolutely everything. Then, you want to clean out each drawer. Vacuum the drawer, and make sure there is nothing spilled or hiding in any of the corners. Once each drawer is cleaned out, decide where you want everything to go. Then, fold your items properly and neatly place them back into your dresser. As you are going through, make sure that everything you have is what you actually want. Anything you don't actually want, you should get rid of. This is especially true with underwear and socks. Often we keep underwear and socks that are torn or that we no longer use and end up having more than we need. Now is the time to throw these away.

If you keep clothes in your closet, you should also go ahead and sort through those. Make sure you actually want what you are keeping and that it is all in good condition. When you are done, you can organize everything back into your closet. Color code everything so that it is easy to find what you are looking for at any given time.

When you are done organizing your dresser and clothes in your closet, you are done with day 7 of your challenge, which commences the end of week one.

Make sure that you put away your daily donation item, and that you fill out your daily journal entry. Then, celebrate that you have successfully worked through to the end of week one!

Day 8
Wu-Men

There are many surfaces in our homes. For untrained individuals, surfaces are a great place for junk to gather and clutter to collect. Today you are going to start something that you will continue doing for the rest of this challenge. So, you will do it for 22 days. That is, you are going to choose one surface per day and completely clean it off. You are going to remove everything from the surface, only replace necessary items, and organize through the rest of the items to put them where they belong.

You may not have 22 surfaces in your home, but there is a good chance a few will need to be redone. It can take the time to instill this habit in your life and make it easier for you to stick to on a daily basis. The goal is to learn how to put things back in their spot and keep your surfaces clear of anything that does not belong to them. You want to discipline yourself to see that a surface doesn't mean more stuff is being welcomed in your home, but that you are finally allowing for clean space to come in your life.

With each surface, you want to clear it off first completely. Wipe it d and make sure that it is nice and clean. Then, if you are going to place a decoration on it, go ahead. Anything else should be organized and put into its respective spot. If there is anything, you don't want to keep, throw it away or put it in your donation box. Do this over and over with all of the surfaces in your home. Make it a goal that you will leave at least half of the surfaces free of anything, even decorations. Having completely clear surfaces is soothing for the mind and emotions, and you will gain much benefit if you learn to keep your surfaces clear and clean on a regular basis.

Once you are done your daily surface, go ahead and do your daily donation item. Then, you can also do your daily journal entry. After you complete these three tasks, you are done day 8 of your 30-day challenge!

Day 9

Today you are going to focus on organizing your photograph collection. This may not be a major problem for you, but many people have a significant number of printed images that they hoard around their home. Younger generations already have the majority of their photographs on a digital platform only, but older generations will need to work through their photographs and organize them.

If you have printed images, you are going to want to sort through them. Any that you don't want to keep should be shredded, and any that you do want to keep should be scanned and uploaded to your computer, and then the hard copy should be shredded. Make sure that all of the files you have on your computer are stored in various places. You can store them directly on your computer itself, to a cloud storage system, and to a USB drive to make sure that they are all safe. If you have any photographs that you *really* want to keep, you can make a photo album or put them in frames around your house.

If you don't have many printed images, these are likely not a major problem for you. However, you likely have a lot of photographs on your digital storage units. Today you are going to go through all of them and delete ones you don't want to keep. Too often we keep all of the pictures we have taken, whether they are good or not. They take up a lot of room, and they end up filling our online albums with photographs we never look at. Instead, delete everything you don't like and organize the remaining ones into relevant photo albums.

After you are done sorting through your photographs, you can do your daily surface, your daily donation item, and your daily journal entry. Then, you are done for day 9 of your 30-day challenge!

Day 10
BCE. Buddha

Day 10 is going to be an easy one. Today, all you must do is relax. You have done wonderful until now, and you deserve to relax. See, one of the many blessings of being a minimalist is that you have less to worry about in your life. You don't have as much cleaning to do; there is not as much stress in your life because you are not worried about maintaining or caring for as many belongings, and you don't have to work as hard to bring new belongings into your home. Today, you are going to revel in that glory.

Make sure that you spend the day relaxing in your favorite way. If you work today, then spend a significant amount of time after work enjoying peace and quiet. Take time to notice all of the advancements you have made and how far you have come in your minimalist journey in the past 10 days. Breathe deeply, meditate, and enjoy a cup of your favorite drink. You can spend today inside of the house or outside of the house; it's completely up to you. You want to do all of the things that make you feel relaxed. There is no right or wrong way to spend this day, as long as you are entering into a state of total relaxation. Then, and only then, have you successfully completed day 10 of your 30-day challenge. After this day, you are one-third of the way done your entire challenge.

Even though you are taking a day for relaxation, be sure to carve out time to clear off one surface, donate one item, and complete one journal entry.

You are halfway done!

Congratulations on making it to the halfway point of the journey. Many try and give up long before even getting to this point, so you are to be congratulated on this. You have shown that you are serious about getting better every day. I am also serious about improving my life, and helping others get better along the way. To do this I need your feedback. Click on the link below and take a moment to let me know how this book has helped you. If you feel there is something missing or something you would like to see differently, I would love to know about it. I want to ensure that as you and I improve, this book continues to improve as well. Thank you for taking the time to ensure that we are all getting the most from each other.

Chapter 3: Days 11 to 20

As you enter into the second leg of your 30-day challenge, you are likely feeling many different emotions. Perhaps you realize that this is easier than you thought it would be, or maybe you are finding it is harder than you initially believed it would be. You might feel a mixture of emotions as you enjoy a clutter-free home but come to terms with the practice of eliminating things you no longer need or want. Perhaps there is still some lingering guilt or regret from eliminating items that you no longer needed or wanted but still held great emotional attachment to. Regardless of what you are feeling, if you have made it into the second leg of your challenge, you are doing a wonderful job. You should take some time to appreciate your success and notice how far you have already come. You are doing great.

For this portion of the challenge, we are going to dig a little deeper. You are going to do more cleaning in the deeper parts of your homes, and you are going to accomplish some harder tasks, like getting rid of items you've been holding onto "just in case". This may bring about even more emotions, but rest assured you will have great success in your journey if you continue following each day as it is laid out for you. If you are ready to begin the second leg of your 30-day challenge, then go ahead and start with day 11. And remember, take your time and be gentle with yourself through this process. It is as much about soul-searching and personal development as it is about cleaning up your home so that you have a clutter-free environment to live in.

Day 11

Today is going to be used for two things if you have a family with young children, or one if you don't. If you have a family with young children, today you are going to focus on the toy collection. Regardless of whether you have a family or not, you are also going to focus on your prized collections.

We are going to start by focusing on the toys if this is applicable to you. Go through every storage container that holds toys and organizes everything. Any toys that are broken should be thrown away. Any toys that are no longer played with should be donated. Children often end up with a bounty of toys, many of which they never use. While it is nice to be able to shower your children with gifts and toys that they long for, it also ends up cluttering up the home. As you are cleaning, think about a few activities you can encourage your children to do without toys involved. Perhaps they might go outside and play pretend, or help bake or do household chores instead. There was a time when children didn't have as many toys as modern children do, and in that time they found ways to occupy themselves without having to own the latest and greatest of gadgets and gear. It is beneficial to encourage your children to do this, as it encourages them to have a greater sense of imagination and learn to manage their time properly. It keeps them from having to rely on toys and such to bring joy into their lives and teaches them to create joy in life.

The second task was to go through your collections. Some of these collections you may be keeping simply because you have invested so much time and perhaps even money into them. It is time to really consider how much you like them and if they are worth it for you to keep them around. Of course, if your collection brings you great joy and it is something that you take pride in, it certainly makes sense to keep it. However, if it does not and you simply did it as a pass time and are now no longer as happy with the collection as you once were, it may be time to let it go.

Once you have dealt with toys and collections, you are ready to move into the daily activities that you are maintaining throughout this challenge. Clean off one surface, put one item in the donation box, and do your daily journaling. If you find that your donation box is becoming full, it is important that you take it directly to the donation drop off location. Do not put it in the garage or somewhere else for storage and simply start a new one. We often fail to actually bring them to the drop off due to procrastination, which is exactly what we don't want.

Day 12

You've probably said it before "yeah, I don't really use it anymore, but I want to hold onto it just in case." If someone were to ask you "just in case what?" you might have a generic answer "well, in case I need it of course!" or you might have no answer at all. Regardless of what your answer might be, it likely isn't a good enough reason to keep storing a bunch of items that you are not currently using.

In many cases, when we see these "just in case" items, it brings us guilt. We think of the things that we feel we should be doing, and feel upset with ourselves that we aren't making time for them anymore. Perhaps the items you are holding onto are ones that you once used frequently or ones that you purchased thinking you would use more than you did. The reality is, these simply make you feel bad for being who you are, and that is never beneficial. Instead of feeling bad and guilty, you are going to eliminate these items and open up space in your life for new things that you are attracted to.

See, in life, we have a tendency to change frequently. Often, our hobbies and interests change on a frequent basis as well. As a result, we can end up with many things that we simply didn't use as often as we thought we might or as often as we used to. In the future, a great idea for working together with your hobbies is only to purchase what you absolutely need.

Or, you might take a class somewhere local so that you can gain access to the supplies available in the class while also learning about the techniques and skills you need to get good at the hobby. If you find that you are still deeply interested in the hobby after a while, then you can go ahead and purchase anything you feel you need to enjoy your hobby fully at home.

Once you have sorted through your "just in case" items and placed them all in boxes, put them directly in your car and take them to the drop-off center. There is no need to store them anywhere where they will end up being forgotten about and staying a part of your household clutter. You need to get rid of them right away.

Complete your daily activities for the challenge, and then you are done for day 12!

Day 13

Today we are going to focus on some digital organization. Previously, you went through all of your photographs online and sorted through them to discover which you wanted to keep and which you wanted to eliminate. You also went through the process of putting them all into neat folders so that they were organized. Today, you are going to do this with the rest of our online belongings.

Because our online belongings are digitized and don't take up physical space, we often overlook them. We forget that they need to be cleaned and maintained in the same way that our other belongings need to be cared for. Because of this, they can become jumbled and confusing, and we can end up losing things in our online world. This can be just as stressful as losing something in the real world.

Today you are going to go through your email, social media accounts, and offline files to organize them all. You are going to put new systems in place that will help you maintain the organization of these devices, and you are going to strictly enforce new rules that will help you keep everything in this organized fashion in the future.

Start with your email. Go back through all of your e-mails and unsubscribe from all of the emails that you receive from stores. You do not need to receive these emails on a frequent basis; they simply encourage you to feel the need to shop and acquire more belongings that you do not need. You then want to delete all unnecessary emails. With all of the remaining emails, you should sort them into appropriate files where you can easily access them if you ever need them.

Next, go onto your social media accounts. Since our social media accounts often go back extremely far, we don't want to waste any time on posts or pictures.

These can remain intact. What you want to focus on are your friend lists. Go through your friend lists and eliminate any friends who you don't actually know, don't talk to, or don't even like. Often we hang on to people on our friend lists because we feel like the overall number reflects how important we are and we attach a great amount of emotional significance to that number and each person on the list, even if we don't actually like them or know them. Today, you are going to eliminate them all and release that emotional burden, freeing yourself up to focus on who actually matters, including yourself.

Finally, you want to organize your offline files. Go through all of the offline files on your computer, make folders for them, and then organize them so that they are easy to find. If there are any that you no longer need, delete them. This frees up space on your computer, and in your mind.

After you are done organizing your online life, go ahead and complete your daily offline tasks. Clear off one surface, put one item in the donation bin, and complete your daily journal entry. Then, you are done for the day.

Day 14

For the last day of week two, we are going to focus on your bedroom. Your bedroom should be your sanctuary. You should feel comfortable, confident, and relaxed any time you are in your bedroom. When you enter this space, you should immediately feel at peace, and like you are in your safe space.

When our bedrooms are cluttered and messy, we carry that as a burden. It increases our stress levels and makes us feel chaotic in our mind. As a result, we often don't sleep soundly, and so we end up suffering physically. Cleaning up your bedroom properly and eliminating clutter from this space can allow you to release all of those tensions and reclaim peace into your life.

To start, look at the obvious. You want to clean off all of the surfaces in the room and sort through everything that you have been storing on them. Then, clear off the floor. Next, clean out all of the drawers. Finally, clean off the bed. If you have a closet, clean this out as well. With each area that you are cleaning, completely remove everything from the space, organize everything, and only replace what absolutely must go back into that space. Everything else should be organized into its new home, donated, or thrown away.

As you are putting your room back together, do it with your comfort and peace in mind. Think about what decorations and accessories will actually enhance the comfort and peace, and let everything else go. Streamline your dressers and nightstands so important things are easily accessible and nothing else can get in the way. Make your bed, but don't replace a ton of pillows or decorations on top of it. These just end up on the floor or shoved aside so that you can access your bed at night. Instead, simply replace what you need and let the rest go.

After you are done reorganizing your room, you can go about your daily tasks of cleaning off one surface, donating one item, and journaling one entry. Then, you are completely done the 14th day of your 30-day challenge. You are also now done your second week of your challenge. You can take this time to celebrate yourself and your accomplishments so far!

Day 15

By now, you have likely found that there are many things in your home that you have considered letting go of but simply aren't able to. You might be realizing how hard it is to let go of the things you love or once loved. Today, we are going to focus on this emotion. We are going to focus on putting a rule in place that will help you work through this emotion in a way that is comfortable and effective.

Today, you are going to learn to sleep on it. Anytime you have something that you aren't sure if you want to keep or let go of, you are going to put it out in the open and then you are going to leave it there until the next day. Sleep on it, think about what you want to do, and then do it. There is no need to get rid of everything in your life. If you are struggling to let it go, sleeping on it will help bring you answers. The next day you will be able to truly decide whether you are struggling because it's difficult to let go of, or if you are struggling because you genuinely don't want to let go of it. Once you have your answer, you can take the appropriate action of either letting go of it, or store it somewhere safe where it can stay organized and remain useful for you.

Remember, the purpose of minimalism isn't to get rid of everything you have and live in barely anything. It is to get rid of the things you no longer need or want and open up space to enjoy the things you do need and want. It allows you freedom from the consumerism life and the opportunity to enjoy yourself beyond your material possessions. It doesn't mean that you can't have material possessions, though. If you love something, but you simply aren't quite sure of whether or not you want to keep it or let go of it, it's time to practice the sleep on it method. You can do this with any and all of the items you have been struggling with until this point in your challenge. You should also do it with any future items that you struggle with.

While you are working on putting this new practice into place, take some time to complete your daily activities. Clean off one surface, put one item in the donation bin, and fill out your daily journal entry.

Day 16

How many items are you keeping because of their sentimental value, and nothing more? Items that a loved one gave you or that once belonged to a loved one, and you hold onto them because of what they resemble you. They might resemble the person themselves, or they might be a symbol of a special time in your life. Old t-shirts, pieces of jewelry, quilts, and more are often kept simply for the sentimental value that they carry.

Sentimental value is a high value, but we often turn it into a higher value than it genuinely needs to be. If you are carrying around sentimental items simply because of their sentimental value and for no other reason, it is the time that you let go of them. If you are not using them and they do not bring you joy daily, or on a regular basis (at least once per week), you should consider letting them go. It is time to clear up space in your life for you to enjoy the things that bring you greater joy than sentimental items.

We often hold onto sentimental items because we feel they are a key to our past. They hold memories or unlock feelings that we worry we may never have again if we don't keep said item around. The reality is, this simply isn't true. You can have any memory or emotion you want without having to have a physical item available to remind you of it. While it can be nice, it can also create clutter.

Having one or two sentimental items is fine, especially if they are ones you use on a regular basis or that bring you joy on a regular basis. But if you are keeping them around simply for what they resemble for you, you need to let them go. If you are really struggling with letting them go, consider taking a picture of them and storing it into a "sentimental items" file on your computer. Then, you can let go of the physical item itself. You will likely feel a great release as you let the past go and open up space in your physical life and in your emotional and psychological life for the future.

Once you are done sorting through and clearing out sentimental items, you can do your daily tasks of cleaning off one surface, donating one item, and journaling your daily entry. Then, you are done for the day.

Day 17

We have been taught that accessories are a major asset to our wardrobe. So much so that we often end up hoarding endless amounts of accessories to accentuate our wardrobe. Massive jewelry collections, hair accessory collections, purse collections, shoe collections and other collections tend to accumulate in our lives as we aspire to be able to create any look we desire at any given moment. In most cases, we don't even wear half of them; we simply have them because we think we may want to use them at some point in the future. It is another classic "just in case" scenario.

Today, you are going to organize your accessory collection. Anything you own that you don't use on a regular basis should be eliminated. You want only to have what you use on a frequent basis left behind. Believe it or not, accessories take up a great amount of space in our homes. We often have so many of them that we end up storing them all over the place in various little boxes and storage contraptions. In many cases, we often even forget what we have, so it never gets used. If you are having this issue, it is time to eliminate them and move on! You need to narrow d your accessory collection to only what you need and nothing more. Let everything else go.

After you are done going through your accessories, you can complete your daily challenge tasks. Then, you are done for the day!

Day 18

Today, you are going to work on a task that might be difficult, but it will also bring great reward. You are going to have an unplugged day. You are going to turn off all of your electronic devices and refrain from using any of them for the rest of the day. TVs, cell phones, radios, computers, tablets and any other electronic devices that you use should all be eliminated for the day. You are going to spend the day doing wholesome real-world activities, free of any electronic distractions.

As a society, we tend to drown ourselves into the world of technology on a daily basis. We are frequently caught up in social media and other online functions as we dissolve hours and hours of time into our electronic devices. While technology is a highly valuable asset in our society, it is also an addictive habit that we must learn to moderate. By taking regular unplugged breaks from the society, we allow ourselves to reset our inner world and have more focus on what is around us. We remind ourselves that there is more to life than the online world, and we are able to reconnect with life itself. It gives us an opportunity to remember what it feels like to live in the now, which can have an incredibly emotional and psychological benefit for our overall wellbeing.

You are encouraged to go a full 24-hours without using any electronic devices today. At the very least, go 12-hours. As you are enjoying your unplugged day, go ahead and complete your three daily tasks so that you accomplish all of your day 18 tasks for the 30-day challenge.

Day 19

The amount of clutter we gather in our kitchens is incredible. We often end up with a number of different gadgets and devices that are used for a variety of different things. Peelers, cork removers, bottle openers, utensils, graters, and several other types of smaller gadgets can build up in our kitchen. We also tend to hoard small appliances that are supposed to make cooking easier. Perhaps you are also hoarding cookbooks, and perhaps even some ingredients that you don't actually use. Today, you are going to sort through them all.

Start with your counters: clear them off and sort through everything you have stored on them. Remember you want to be throwing things away, donating some, and only keeping what you really want and need. Anything you don't use on a regular basis should not be considered a want or need, no matter how handy or useful the device has the potential to be. After you do your counters, go into your drawers. Then, go into your cupboards. Finally, organize the contents of your fridge. You want to completely organize everything in all of these areas so that when you are using your kitchen for cooking, you no longer have to sort through piles and piles of junk. Instead, you can simply find everything you actually need with an easy glance.

Make sure that when you are replacing the contents of your kitchen back into their respective homes that you are being organized about it. Designate a single purpose for each cupboard or shelf and drawer. Then, only return items that actually fulfill those purposeful needs into those areas. You might consider creating "sections" of your kitchen to help you choose a purpose. For example, you might keep serving dishes, cookware and cooking utensils near the stove, dishes and utensils near the sink, and storage devices near the fridge. By creating these different sections within' your kitchen, you make it extremely easy to know where things should be placed. You also make it easy to access what you need from whichever appliance you are working next to.

The final thing you should do in your kitchen is to sweep and mop the floors and clean out your sink. Freshen it up, open the window, and let in some natural lighting. This will help your kitchen feel cleaner and more welcoming. When you are done, complete your daily challenge tasks. Then, you are all done with day 19 of your 30-day challenge!

Day 20

You may not have noticed previously, but you likely store a ton of things on the floor. Look in obvious sight, and look in less obvious sight. You might be surprised to see how many things are being hidden in plain sight. Today, you are going to focus on clearing your floors and cleaning them up properly. Your end goal will be to have floors that can be vacuumed, swept, or mopped effortlessly without having to clean before you do these tasks.

You are going to go through every room in your house to do this. Start in one room, and work your way through the rest. Carry a garbage bag, a donation box, and cleaning supplies from room to room. You want to pull everything off the floor. Throw things away, donate what you no longer need or want, and organize what you want to keep. As you finish in each room, clean the floor completely. You should be able to clean the floor without having to lift, clean, or move anything off the floor. In other words, all of the trash and unwanted items should be gone, and all of the items that are being kept should be properly stored away in their unique homes that aren't on the floor.

When you have completed this task, you may complete your daily challenge tasks. This will mark the end of day 20 and the end of your second leg of the challenge. After this, there are only 10 days left!

Chapter 4: Days 21 to 30

You are officially entering the last leg of the 30-day challenge. Starting today, you will be completing the last 10 days of the challenge, and then you will be done. For the end of your challenge, we are going to be gentle but persistent. You are going to get the rest of your house in order, and you are going to work on your inner world as well. By the end of this leg you should feel refreshed and rejuvenated, and you should be able to look around your house and see peace and comfort, instead of chaos and clutter.

If you have made it this far, you should celebrate yourself. Minimalism is an easy lifestyle, but it isn't always easy to transition into this lifestyle. You want to always congratulate yourself and celebrate your successes as you make any large changes in your lifestyle. After all, if you have made it this far then you are doing a wonderful job. You deserve to feel happy and joyful about your accomplishments and take pride in your success.

Day 21

Today you are primarily going to focus on your daily tasks. You are going to take it easy and focus on your inner world and wellbeing. You are going to breathe, meditate, and take it slow. Remember, this challenge is not intended to be tough or to shock you into a new way of life. You want it to be refreshing, rejuvenating, and effortless. You want to feel good as you complete each task, and feel confident as you embrace your new lifestyle. The easier you are on yourself, the more you will enjoy the transformation, and the more likely the new lifestyle will stick, and you won't end up reverting back to old habits after this challenge is completed.

Take some time today to completely relax. Do whatever make you feel at total peace, and nurture your inner world. You are also going to take some time to look back at your emotions over the challenge so far. Think about times that were difficult, and think about how the end result made you feel. Think about where you have experienced resistance or struggle, and notice what it felt like to work through those emotions. Or, if you are still carrying them, take some time to work through those emotions.

Today is all about taking care of yourself and nurturing your inner space. A major part of minimalism is learning to nurture ourselves and take care of our inner world. It is important that you take the time to embrace this part of the lifestyle change when you are in the process of transforming your life to one of a minimalist. As your physical world declutters and frees itself from emotional burdens and setbacks, it should become easier for your psychological and emotional worlds to do the same.

Take your time, go slowly, and enjoy each part of today. Don't forget to do your daily challenge tasks. In addition, you are going to add a new daily task. You are going to spend at least 20 minutes per day allowing yourself to relax and enjoy the moment completely.

Day 22

The addition of electronics in our world has been a wonderful one, but it has also brought about a great deal of clutter. Think about how many belongings you have that are electronics or that are accessories for your electronics. Remotes, cases, batteries, cords, and more can all become clutter when we aren't actively maintaining them and keeping them organized and properly stored away.

Today, you are going to focus on cleaning up your electronic devices. Any accessories will need to find a proper home, and devices themselves will be stored properly as well. Smaller devices can be stored neatly in drawers, and larger devices should be kept in a tidy and organized space. If you have a TV stand, for example, take some time to organize the stand and make sure that anything on top of it is neat and tidy and is resting where it is supposed to. You also want to take a look at the cords. Do some cord management by tying up loose ends and keeping them streamlined. The more organized your cords are, the neater your electronics will look.

After you are done, complete your four daily tasks: relax for 20 minutes, donate a daily item, clear off a surface, and complete your daily journal entry. Then, you are done for day 22.

Day 23

Today you are going to start a week-long challenge that you will use for the rest of the 30-day challenge. This challenge might be tough, but you can certainly do it. You are not going to spend money for an entire week, outside of necessities like gas and groceries. You will not purchase fast food or eat at restaurants, purchase clothes or other unnecessary items, nor will you spend money on anything else. You are going to refrain from purchasing anything at all this week.

We spend money faster than we make money in this society, and it leads to a negative cycle that can be hard to break. In many cases, we don't even realize how much money we are spending until it is all gone. You are going to start changing this cycle by taking this week off from spending any more money. The amount you will save from not shopping will be incredible.

We often don't realize that we are spending our money. And in some cases, we don't know how much we are spending over time. We buy a shirt here, a pair of pants there, a bag of chips here and drink from our favorite coffee house there. We spend a little bit at a time, and we forget about how much it all amounts to when we are done. It leads to a negative cycle where we are constantly eating through any money we might have. It also leads to using bringing home a significant amount of clutter that we don't actually need. In many cases, the trinkets we are buying and bringing home aren't things we actually wanted. Instead, they are impulse purchases we made that were intended to help us feel better about something in our lives that we may be feeling unhappy about. Stress, anger, sadness, and other emotions can lead us to spend money impulsively. We must learn different coping methods if we are going to save money and refrain from bringing home any extra and unnecessary junk.

So, put your money aside and stop spending starting today. You will keep this up for one week. Don't forget to complete your daily challenge tasks so that you can successfully complete day 23 of your challenge!

Day 24

Today, you are going to be kind to yourself. You are going to spend an entire day without judging yourself or speaking harshly to yourself. You will not engage in any negative self-speak. Instead, you are going to practice working on positive self-talk and start developing a positive relationship with yourself.

With the rise of consumerism has come an even greater rise of self-doubt and self-criticism. We see billboards and major campaigns that show us who we are supposed to be, and when we realize we aren't that person we begin engaging in self-doubt and negative self-talk. We question ourselves and what must be wrong with us, and we fail to be kind to ourselves. It can be extremely damaging on our emotional, psychological and often indirectly on our physical wellbeing. It is important that we learn to love ourselves as we are and be kind to ourselves. When we learn to be this way, we can lead a more peaceful and positive life.

Today, anytime you notice you are harsh or judgmental towards yourself, you are simply going to change your thoughts to "I love, honor, and respect myself." There is no need to punish or criticize yourself for the negative feedback, as this would go against the purpose of today's challenge. Simply be kind and gently direct yourself back on track for your daily tasks.

At some point throughout the day, be sure to complete your four daily challenge tasks. Spend 20 minutes relaxing, clear off a surface, donate one item, and complete your daily journal entry.

Day 25

When we no longer have to worry about investing time into acquiring and maintaining our physical possessions, we free up a great amount of time to begin enjoying our lives. Today, you are going to start enjoying that free time. You are going to try something new that you have never done before.

Trying something new can be something small and simple, or it can be something large and extensive. You can do something as simple as trying a new beverage or taking a new class, or you can try something incredible like skydiving or scuba diving. Whatever you choose to do, try and make it something that you've always wanted to try but never felt that you had the time to complete. Or, if you truly don't have the time today to complete that one thing, schedule a time to do it and book all of the necessary appointments you need to complete that task and do something smaller for today.

When we try new things, we open our minds to the world of possibility. We exercise our freedom and our right to be who we want to be, and the outcome can be extremely liberating. It is important that you try new things on a regular basis, as this will allow you to keep yourself from feeling mundane and trapped in a world of routine where days melt into each other and time seems unimportant and irrelevant.

After you are doing trying something new, do your daily challenge tasks. Then, you are all done for day 25 of your 30-day challenge!

Day 26

Today you are going to do another task that has nothing to do with material belongings. You are going to spend an entire day without complaining. For one 24-hour period, you are not going to complain about anything at all. You won't complain about time, traffic, inconveniences, people, or anything else that you might feel compelled to complain about. You will simply appreciate life whenever and wherever you can, and stay quiet and calm in moments where you feel stressed, and like you want to complain about something.

When we complain out loud, we reinforce the negative thoughts we have in our heads. It can create a terrible downward spiral of frequent negative thoughts that arrive in similar situations, and before we know it, we are trapped in negative habits that can hold us back and keep us from experiencing true joy in life. When we learn to refrain from outwardly experiencing these negative thoughts and emotions, we learn to deal with them inwardly in a more positive method as well. The outcome can be liberation from negative thoughts and lasting negative emotions. We learn to embrace life, go with the flow, and accept that not everything will happen in the most convenient manner possible. It is one of the greatest lessons you can teach yourself.

In addition to not complaining about 24-hours, you should complete your daily challenge tasks. Spend 20 minutes relaxing, clear off one surface, donate one item, and write your daily journal entry.

Day 27

Many people hoard books, which can turn into us having massive collections of titles that we have read but will likely never look at again. Books are valuable, and the knowledge they offer us is unparalleled. However, they also take up a lot of space and can become overwhelming and difficult to store over time. Today, you are going to focus on narrowing your book collection.

There are several ways to improve your book collection, but first, you are going to start with what you have on hand. Start by going through every book you have and putting the ones you will never read again into a donate bin. Even if you loved the book, donate it. There is no benefit in storing it if you will never read it again. Donate the books immediately after you are done taking them off the shelf. Then, organize what you have left.

To refrain from building up another massive book collection, try one or both of these methods: purchase digital books, or borrow from the library. Digital books are a wonderful opportunity to own titles without having them take up space in your physical world. You can purchase any title you want and have it kept in an online library where you can simply read at your will. You can read it on any digital device you have that allows you to download the appropriate reading application to read your titles. Borrowing books from a library is another great option. Some people still prefer to read a physical book, which is fine. However, purchasing books simply to have the ability to read them physically is quite redundant, especially if you will never read the book again. Instead, borrow from the library.

Once you are done organizing your book collection, you can then complete your daily challenge tasks. Then, you are done for the day!

Day 28

Today, you are going to sort through your toiletries and eliminate unnecessary belongings. You might be surprised to realize how much you have hoarded in your bathroom, as we tend to keep all sorts of different toiletries on hand. Hair products, bath products, skin products, makeup, medicines, and other toiletries tend to build up in our bathrooms. If we aren't careful, our drawers and cupboards can begin to overflow, and we will no longer have space for all of our belongings.

Start by emptying everything out of your shower, cupboards, drawers, medicine cabinet and counters and putting them into a bin. Then, clean everything d thoroughly. Make sure any spills, grime, or build up is eliminated before you start putting your bathroom back together. Next, have a garbage bag handy. Go through every single item in the bin. Anything that you do not use or want should be thrown away. Anything that you are keeping should be stored in its respective home for you to easily access when you need it. If you find you have too many belongings or it still doesn't look organized when you are done, consider getting drawer organizers and caddies for the cupboards to help you keep everything organized and in its designated place.

When you are done, complete your daily challenge tasks.

Day 29

Today, you are going to clean out your wallet and, if you have one, your purse. We often store many things in our wallets and purses that we don't need to carry around with us. The primary culprit is unneeded cards. Club cards, points cards, and even hotel keys or gift cards can take up a massive amount of space in our wallets. In purses, all sorts of things can pile up. It is time to sort through these and organize them completely.

Take the time to go through all of your cards and everything else inside of your wallet and purse and organize it properly. Throw things away, put items where they belong, and take inventory of what you have. If you have unused gift cards or store credit cards, take this as an opportunity to use them or sell them. There is no need to carry these around if you are never going to actually use them.

Once you are done, complete your daily challenge tasks. Write in your journal, take 20 minutes to relax, clear off one surface, and donate one item.

Day 30

For the final day of your challenge, you are going to clean out your car. Our cars tend to become a mobile storage facility that carries everything that we forget to bring inside or throw away. It is time to get a proper system in place so that you can have your car be clean and organized for when you are inside of it.

Start by taking a garbage bag and a bin into your car. Throw every piece of trash away, and throw everything else into the bin. When you are done, vacuum out your car and wash off your floor mats. Replace your scented air fresheners and anything else in your car that helps keep it feeling and smelling clean. If you have kids in the car or tend to carry a lot around for business, consider investing in over-the-seat organizers or bins for your trunk that will help keep everything organized properly. Then, replace anything that needs to be in your car back into its appropriate home. Everything else should be brought inside and organized into its respective spot within your house.

You should clean out your car on a regular basis to prevent it from piling up with junk and garbage that you do not need to be carrying around with you each day.

When you are done, complete your daily tasks of cleaning off one surface, relaxing for 20 minutes, donating one item, and doing your daily journal entry. Since it is the last day of your challenge, you should also go ahead and bring your donation bin to the donation drop off center.

Book 4: Essential Oils

Essential Oils for beginners your guide to healing with aromatherapy and essential oil recipes for beauty and health

By

Beatrice Anahata

Do you like essential oils?

Essential oils are something that many people seem to love to try, and they have a wide variety of different uses. But, what are the best ones? What are the best ways to use them? What are the best benefits that you can get from these different oils, and how complex is it to use these invaluable oils on your body and in your home?

Obviously, they can help our body in a ton of different means, but at the same time, you might wonder what the best ones to use are, and what the best uses for these are. Well, you're about to find out.

Essential oils can typically be used either topically, in a diffuser, diluted with a carrier oil such as coconut or olive oil, or they can be used in water or other cleansers to help spray it into an area. There are so many different ways to use these and often, you probably feel overwhelmed as to what does what. Well, let's go over just what extent these essential oils can help you.

This chapter will go into detail on how you can use essential oils, including the top benefits for this. They're very simple to use, and you can get started with these right away. By using them, you'll be able to have a better home for yourself, and for others, and from there, you'll be able to create a better life for yourself too. Natural medicine can really help you out, and essential oils are definitely the way to go. You'll be able to learn about the top benefits here, and what oils you can use to accomplish these various measures to help your life.

BASIC RECIPES

We typically recommend the following:

if you are going to use a topical (a blended recipe smoothed on the body with an oil or cream, or essential oils on a compress, or "neat" for instance), always inhale it directly first. Bioavailability is better with inhalation, meaning more effective and swifter action in that route, but in many instances, topical is also useful as it works slower and lasts longer the skin. In other words, for most applications calling for a topical, it makes sense to also inhale.

INSOMNIA

- Simply diffuse lavender at night in the bedroom. Simplicity at its best. In addition, you could add a few lavender drops to your washing machine when you wash your sheets and pillowcases; you could put a few drops of lavender on a cotton ball or in a sachet and tuck it under the pillow.
- Blend 10 drops lavender, 10 drops Roman chamomile, 4 drops vetiver and 4 drops clary sage in an ounce of carrier oil. Apply on neck, wrists and feet at night and inhale or diffuse. (I

like to use the rollerball applicators in a glass bottle – easy when you are tired at night and effective.)
- Buy a premade Sleep Blend. Many companies offer them (including mine). Our Zen Sublime Sleep is blended in an organic carrier oil so it can be applied to your skin as well as inhaled or diffused. Here is the blend and why I chose each EO:

    o Lavender – well known and most used essential oil for sleep assistance. Lavender calms, soothes and nurtures. It helps to balance the spirit, and reduces any existing anxiety. It also helps reduce pains which may hinder sleep.
    o Rose Geranium – fosters a sense of security and protects from disturbing energy or thoughts.
    o Orange – unblocks energy; found in clinical tests to be a sedative that calms, pushes down pessimism and is a tonic for mind and body.
    o Neroli – relaxes nerves, soothes the heart and psyche, and helps relieve pain.
    o Cedarwood – is very grounding, a tonic for the nervous system and is of course anti-inflammatory.

- Clary Sage – well-known to reduce anxiety and stress, which may be the cause of sleeplessness. It works synergistically with lavender for sedation and calming effect.

Sore Throat

- Do a steam inhalation of 2 drops Chamomile, 3 drops Lavender and 1 drop Thyme.
- For simplicity, do a steam inhalation of just 2 drops Clove.
- After a steam inhalation, massage the blend of 2 drops Lemon, 1 drop Thyme and 4 drops Chamomile in a tablespoon of a carrier oil onto your throat and neck (including behind your ears.)
- (From Aromahead) Put one drop of Tea Tree in a glass of warm water, mix it, and then gargle. Don't worry if you swallow a little, but try to spit out most of it. Gargle like this several times a day. You can also put one drop of Sandalwood in a bit of jojoba and rub it on the front and back of your neck.
- Make this blend to inhale or diffuse every 3 hours. 12 drops lavender, 6 drops black pepper and 3 drops myrrh.
- Buy a premade blend. There are many available!

- I personally find that if a sore throat is making it's appearance and hasn't really taken hold, I inhale Eucalyptus every hour (and sometimes I will also inhale myrrh and/or clove) and it goes away.

Tonsillitis

- Blend in 2 teaspoons of a carrier oil 6 drops Rose Geranium, 4 drops Myrrh and 2 drops Orange or Sweet Orange. Massage on the throat and neck, and inhale.
- Put 1 drop of Tea Tree in 1 tsp of honey plus 1 cup of warm water, mix well then gargle (do not swallow.)

Cough

- Blend 2 drops Eucalyptus, 2 drops lemon and 1 drop Tea Tree in 2 teaspoons honey. Dilute in a cup of warm water and gargle.
- For a spasmodic cough: blend 2 drops Cypress and 1 drop Frankincense on a cotton ball or tissue, inhale deeply.
- For a spasmodic cough (from Aromahead): blend 5 drops Black Pepper, 5 drops Frankincense and 5 drops Black Spruce in a personal handheld inhaler. Use as needed.

- Dry cough: Mix Eucalyptus 3 drops, and Thyme 2 drops in 1 teaspoon of a carrier, massage on chest and throat.
- Blend Eucalyptus, Cedarwood, Pine and Myrrh in 1/6 ounce bottle. Inhale, use in a diffuser or tent steam; or mix with a carrier oil 1 ounce and massage on the throat.

Tooth Ache

- Dot Clove onto a Q-tip and touch the affected area. It will help reduce pain and inflammation.

Congestion

- Do a Eucalyptus steam. Add 10 drops of Eucalyptus and 10 drops of Siberian Fir Needle with 8 drops of Tea Tree and 2 drops Myrrh to boiling water. Make a steam tent with a towel and inhale with eyes closed.
- Put 2-4 drops of Eucalyptus in the corner of your shower in the morning, and let the steam rise and help you. Make sure to put the drops where you won't stand or step to avoid slipping.
- Blend Eucalyptus, Myrrh, Peppermint and Lemon or diffuse any one of these (your choice) to help break up congestion and breathe better. They will also clarify the air.

- Buy a premade blend that can be massaged on your chest and throat as well as inhaled. Ours is blended in organic jojoba and sunflower and includes:
- Eucalyptus - well-known and wide ranging benefits, including sinus and respiratory applications, increases blood flow and helps with mental exhaustion. It is known to be anti-inflammatory, antispasmodic and very importantly, a decongestant.
- Rosemary - In addition decreasing the levels of cortisol (a stress hormone which can kick in when you are sick which hurts the immune system), Rosemary oil has properties believed to be helpful in relieving respiratory issues and reducing pain.
- Juniper Berry - among its many qualities, Juniper Berry is a detoxifier or purifier of blood, helping to remove toxins.
- Lime - Limes, like lemons, are full of antioxidants, bactericides and other beneficial nutrients. It helps to fight and protect against viral infections which may cause the common cold. Additionally, lime is an antiseptic, meaning it can cure infections and protect against their development.

Headache

- There are different types of headaches, from a sinus headache, migraine to a tension headache. Here are a few suggestions:
- For many types of headaches, use a cool compress or washcloth. Swish the cloth in cool water with 2 drops lavender and 1 drop peppermint, or 2 drops lavender and 1 drop Rose Geranium (inhale to see what you react to better). Put the cold compress on your forehead and relax in a darkened room.
- General headache for no reason: 3 drops Lavender and 1 drop peppermint, use neat or blend in 1 tsp of a carrier. Apply and massage around the temples, back of neck and around the hairline (be sure to patch test first any EO used neat.)
- Nervous headache: 3 drops lavender and 2 drops chamomile or an alternative is 1 drop Rose Geranium, 2 drops lemon and 3 drops lavender in 1 tsp of a carrier. Massage in and relax.
- Sinus headache: steam inhale 3 drops rosemary, 1 drop thyme and 1 drop peppermint or eucalyptus.
- Acute sinusitis: Combine 4 drops eucalyptus, lavender, peppermint, pine and tea tree in a bowl, drop in a wick for an inhaler or cotton

balls, then place inside the personal inhaler and use 5 times a day.
- Do the same recipe but only 1 drop of each in hot water and do a steam inhalation.
- In a pinch, inhale eucalyptus directly from the bottle frequently.
- Tension headache: Blend into 1 ounce of cream 3 drops lavender, 4 drops Frankincense, 1 drop Rosemary and 1 drop Helichrysum. Run on the back of your neck and temples when tension begins.
- General headache: Put 4 drops of lemon in 1 tsp of carrier, and drop in a bath and relax in the tub.
- Buy a premade blend, made by many companies.

Anxiety Attack

- Blend 10 drops each of Lavender, Geranium and Rosemary and diffuse or inhale.
- Blend Neroli 7 drops, Lavender 3 drops and Lemon 20 drops; diffuse.
- For guilt & depression that spurs anxiety: 15 drops Rose Geranium, 10 drops Bergamot, Lavender 5 drops, Turmeric 5 drops; diffuse.
- Inhale or diffuse Rosemary or Lavender alone.

Plain Old Stress

- Blend 3 drops Lavender, 3 drops Bergamot, 1 drop Rose Geranium and 1 drop Frankincense in a diffuser or personal inhaler.
- Blend 3 drops of Clary Sage, 1 drop of Lemon and 1 drop Lavender in your diffuser or personal inhaler.
- Massage Blend. Blend into 1 ounce of a carrier oil 5 drops Cedarwood, 5 drops Bergamot, 2 drops Jasmine or Ylang Ylang and 1 drop Neroli.
- Buy a premade blend. We love ours – Zen De-Stress is blended in organic jojoba and sunflower oil, and includes:
    - Lavender – lavender essential oil has the ability to eliminate nervous tension, relieve and calm. The refreshing aroma also helps with nervous exhaustion and helps lower blood pressure.
    - Clary Sage – is an anti-depressant among its many powers. It helps fight depression and relieves anxiety while helping to boost joy.
    - Neroli – is also an anti-depressant along with holding sedative powers. It helps drive away sadness and lifts the mood (which is why this oil is

extensively used in Aromatherapy techniques.)
- Roman Chamomile – is excellent for combating stress, and helps those who are depressed, lonely or fearful. It helps calm, and is also good for times of anger or irritability.

TUMMY RUB FOR CONSTIPATION
(From Aromahead)

- Blend into 1 ounce of cream 7 drops Sweet Marjoram, 3 drops Bergamot, 3 drops Orange, 2 drops Neroli, 1 drop Roman Chamomile and 5 drops Spikenard. Massage on tummy several times daily.

TUMMY RUB FOR IBS OR CRAMPS
(From Aromahead)

- Blend into 2 ounces of a cream 5 drops of Orange, 5 drops Roman Chamomile, 5 drops Sandalwood and 4 drops Bergamot. Massage on belly and lower back every few hours.
- Blend 6 drops Turmeric into a carrier oil. (Add 2 drops Bergamot if desired) Massage on tummy.
- Blend 2-3 drops Clove and 4 drops Roman Chamomille into a carrier oil and massage onto your tummy. Can also help relieve gas

Bliss And Relaxation

- For an uplifting yet blissful feeling, blend into 1 ounce of cream or oil 2 drops Rose Geranium, 2 drops Bergamot, 1 drop Orange.
- Buy a premade blend. Our Zen Air Bliss contains: Ylang Ylang, Sweet Orange, Bergamot, Magnolia and Neroli.

Muscle Pain And Stiffness

- Blend into 1 ounce of a carrier like jojoba or baobab: 4 drops Eucalyptus, 4 drops Black Pepper, 4 drops Lavender and 2 drops Rosemary. Rub on the affected area as needed (every 2 hours when there is acute pain.)
- You can put the same recipe on a compress without the carrier (cool or warm). Drop the essential oils into a bowl of water (heated or cooled), swish your cloth in it, wring out and apply. For extra power, put your carrier solution on the skin; then apply the compress.

Swollen Muscles And Joints

- Blend into 1 ounce of a carrier oil 8 drops Roman Chamomile, 3 drops Lavender, 4 drops Frankincense, 3 drops Helichrysum.
- Simplicity for arthritis or rheumatoid arthritis: use Frankincense or Turmeric, or blend both in an oil or cream; twice daily, massage into the

affected joints. Diffuse Frankincense or Turmeric when desired.

Cuts

- Put 1-2 drops of Lavender neat on the cut, or
- Put 1-2 drops of Helichrysum neat on the cut, or
- Put 1-2 drops of Rose Geranium on the cut.
- Each will serve as an antibacterial and healing agent. Rose Geranium has a clotting action and helps stop the bleeding. (I keep these 3 in the kitchen for handy use.) Turmeric does the same thing, and is good as a followup for healing in a gel or cream.

Leg Cramps

- Blend 2 drops Peppermint, 4 drops Cypress, 2 drops Ginger, and 2 drops Sweet Marjoram with 4 teaspoons carrier oil of your choice and massage in.
- Blend into 15 ml of Coconut oil or other carrier oil 5 drops Rosemary oil, 3 drops Lavender oil, 2 drops Turmeric and 6 drops Marjoram oil. Massage in circular motions.
- In a pinch, simply blend Peppermint in jojoba oil and massage in.

- Check if your calcium, magnesium and potassium levels are off or not in balance. This could cause cramps, among other things.

Cold Sores

- (courtesy Aromahead.) Blend 30 drops Sandalwood and 3 drops Eucalyptus radiate into 1 ounce of aloe vera gel. Dab it on the cold sore or area where it is developing ever hour.

Acne

- Tea Tree and Juniper Berry are two essential oils that have been studied and tested with acne. Tea Tree is effective on acne and oily skin, and juniper berry is a good antibacterial for acne.
- Tea Tree could be used "neat" but do the patch test first. Simply drop 2-3 drops of Tea Tree onto the acne or pimple twice daily. Otherwise, blend into jojoba which works with well with the skin.
- Blend Tea Tree and Juniper into an aloe gel or jojoba oil, and use as a serum to tamp down oil and breakouts.

PESTS (Mice, Rats, Cockroaches)
- These pests hate or fear Peppermint. Put 4-5 drops of Peppermint on a tea bag and place at the back of kitchen cabinets or where there may be holes in the wall or cabinets (points of entry) as a deterrent. Likewise, Clove is helpful against spiders and bugs. Make sure your dog or cat can't get at the tea bag!

Refreshing Your Home

We have mentioned some uses throughout the book. Here are just a few of them:
- Put 2 drops of Lavender in your washing machine or a 1 drop on the dryer cloth when doing bed linens – or any laundry!
- Put 1 drop of Lavender in your dishwasher to help disinfect and freshen.
- Use your favorite essential oil (Lemon, Lime or Bergamot work well) to wipe down surfaces. Put drops into spray bottle with water or white vinegar.
- Use Tea Tree on a paper towel to wipe around areas that get fungi or mold (inside hidden areas of washer, drains, bathroom corners.
- Diffuse your favorite essential oils in various rooms for various situation, such as: energetic children at night – diffuse lavender an hour before bedtime (and in the bedroom if

desired). Sick ones at home – diffuse clove or eucalyptus or lemon. Want a tranquil environment – diffuse frankincense. A joyful one – do a blend like Zen Bliss, or diffuse sweet orange, ylang ylang, frankincense or bergamot. Grieving – diffuse Rose Geranium. Diffuse your favorite essential oil.
- There are hundreds more recipes and uses for essential oils, and I hope this has given you a jumping off point!

Go Wild With Wild Orange

One essential oil that is actually great for many home remedies, including nervous system issues, is wild orange. The first thing that you'll notice the second that you have this is that it smells utterly amazing, and most people love this for the smell alone. However, did you know that there are so many properties that you can use this for? Did you know that you can use it to help with inflammation, bacteria, digestive system issues, and even to help with sedation? That's right, it works for all of these, and it can definitely help you in your everyday life. You can go wild with wild orange, and it contains most of the benefits that essential oils can give to you.

It's also a means to help really kill bacteria. By diffusing a few drops into a space, it will directly kill bacteria.

Now, if you do choose to use this on the skin, wait about 6 hours before you go out into the sun since it can cause a sensitivity, and it might burn the skin.

If you want an essential oil that smells good and contains a lot of the medical benefits that you're looking for, then look no further for wild orange is ready to go and save the day. Have this, use this on the body, and from there, you can reap the benefits of this on the system, and it'll allow you to have a much better life as a result from this.

Acne

Thanks to medical science, we know that acne is a skin condition aggravated by hormonal changes in the body—and not a reaction to chocolate. Cleansing the skin properly helps those stricken with blemishes fight the production of sebum, the oily substance that clogs pores. Replicated studies in Australia and India have determined that tea tree essential oil is as effective at fighting acne (killing the specific bacteria that cause acne) as the pharmaceutical benzoyl peroxide, so you can battle a breakout with a natural, cost-effective remedy.

Neat Acne Swab

Makes 1 treatment

2 drops tea tree essential oil

1. In the morning, wash your face with mild soap and water, and dry with a clean towel.
2. Place 2 drops of tea tree essential oil on a cotton swab or cotton ball.
3. Gently dab each pimple with the cotton swab or ball.

Acne Night Treatment

Makes 10 treatments

30 drops orange essential oil

15 drops carrot seed essential oil

5 drops juniper essential oil

5 drops Roman chamomile essential oil

1. In a small glass or metal bowl, mix the orange, carrot seed, juniper, and Roman chamomile essential oils neat (undiluted), and pour the mixture into a small (5-mL) dark amber or cobalt glass bottle. Close the bottle tightly and keep it closed until you are ready to use the blend.
2. Before bed, place 5 drops of the oil blend on a cotton swab or cotton ball and rub over your acne. Leave it on for 5 minutes, then dab off any excess with a tissue.
3. Apply nightly until the acne fades. Store the remaining blend in a cool place out of direct sunlight.

Aging Skin

Excessive sun exposure, smoking, or a diet low in antioxidants can all cause skin to age sooner and more rapidly than we would like. The astringent and regenerative properties of essential oils can renew your skin and help slow the aging process. I've chosen sweet almond oil and jojoba oil for carrier oils because of their soft texture, moisturizing effects, and pleasant scents.

Aging Skin Tightening Rub

Makes 4 to 8 treatments

2 tablespoons sweet almond oil

12 drops sandalwood essential oil

8 drops geranium essential oil

1. In a small glass or metal bowl, combine the sweet almond oil with the sandalwood and geranium essential oils. Store in a 1-ounce dark amber or cobalt glass bottle.
2. After cleansing your skin, smooth 1 teaspoon of this blend onto your face and neck.

3. Use once daily. Store the remaining blend in a cool place out of direct sunlight.

Aging Skin Eye Wrinkle Defense

Makes 6 to 9 treatments

6 tablespoons jojoba oil

30 drops myrrh essential oil

1. In a 4-ounce dark amber or cobalt glass jar, combine the jojoba oil and myrrh essential oil. Cap the jar and shake well to combine.
2. Using the tip of your finger, or with a cotton swab, gently apply a few drops to the skin under your eyes and massage until the oil is absorbed.
3. Use once daily. Store the remaining blend in a cool place out of direct sunlight.

Air Freshener

How does that stale smell come into your home? If you have to keep windows closed during a long winter, you can still freshen the air indoors with essential oils. A simple mix of these oils with water will provide enough natural deodorizing power to keep you from spending money on perfumed chemical-based air fresheners.

Pine Air Freshener Spray

Makes 16 ounces

2 cups water

16 drops eucalyptus essential oil

16 drops pine essential oil

16 drops tea tree essential oil

1. In a pint-size glass or metal spray bottle, combine the water with the eucalyptus, pine, and tea tree essential oils. Cap the bottle and shake well to combine.

2. Mist this freshener around your house wherever—and whenever— it will do some good.
3. Store the remaining blend in a cool place out of direct sunlight.

NOTE: In addition to the essential oils used in this recipe, many other essential oil combinations will work, too: lemon and eucalyptus for a clean scent, or orange, clove, and sandalwood for warm, bright notes.

Anger

How often do we hear that we should step back and take a deep breath when something makes us angry? Here's a way to make that pause to breathe as effective as possible: Scent it with the calming effects of aromatherapy. These recipes will help you find the fragrances that bring you back to earth, whether you use them at home, in the car, or at the office.

Anger Diffuser Treatment

Makes 1 diffusion

3 drops chamomile (German or Roman) essential oil

3 drops balsam fir essential oil

3 drops rose essential oil

3 drops sandalwood essential oil

1. To the water in your diffuser, add the chamomile, balsam fir, rose, and sandalwood essential oils, and turn it on. Let the diffuser run for at least 15 minutes. Breathe.

Anger Spray Blend

Makes 1 ounce

2 tablespoons distilled water

3 drops lavender essential oil

1 drop clary sage essential oil

1 drop galbanum essential oil

1 drop peppermint essential oil

1. In a 1-ounce glass or metal spray bottle, combine the water with the lavender, clary sage, galbanum, and peppermint essential oils. Cap the bottle and shake well to combine.
2. Spray this blend at home, in the car, or use it (judiciously) in an area of your workplace where you can enjoy it without objection from your coworkers. If you have an office with a door, close the door before spraying.
3. Store the remaining blend in a cool place out of direct sunlight until you need it again.

Anxiety

Many essential oils can help ease the anxiousness that comes with daily work and life. The solutions suggested here can bring relaxation and release when the day's events overwhelm your sense of well-being. Milk aids the oils' absorption into the bath water, so they don't float on top.

Anxiety-Releasing Bath

Makes 1 treatment

½ cup milk

4 drops sandalwood essential oil

1 drop ylang-ylang essential oil

In a small glass or metal bowl, mix the milk with the sandalwood and ylang-ylang essential oils.

Run a warm bath and then add the milk and oils to the warm water.

Step in, breathe in the scents, and relax.

Anxiety-Reducing Spray

Makes 2 ounces

4 tablespoons distilled water

6 drops lavender essential oil

2 drops cedarwood essential oil

2 drops geranium essential oil

2 drops spearmint essential oil

1. In a 4-ounce glass or metal spray bottle, mix the water with the lavender, cedarwood, geranium, and spearmint essential oils. Cap the bottle and shake well to combine.
2. Spray 2 or 3 pumps in your home or car, as needed.
3. Store the remaining blend in a cool place out of direct sunlight. Remember to shake again before each use.

Arthritis

Wherever the pain of arthritis strikes, a topical application of essential oils with their anti-inflammatory properties can help bring relief to stiff, aching joints. Clove and sandalwood essential oils can also provide penetrating pain relief. In addition to Biblical essential oils, add evening primrose, a carrier oil that is one of nature's most effective anti-inflammatory oils. If evening primrose is not available, jojoba oil or sweet almond oil are good substitutes.

Arthritis Pain Relief Rub

Makes 6 treatments

2 tablespoons evening primrose oil

15 drops clove essential oil

15 drops sandalwood essential oil

1. In a 2-ounce dark amber or cobalt glass bottle, mix the evening primrose oil with the clove and sandalwood essential oils. Cap the bottle and shake well to combine.
2. Apply about 1 teaspoon of this mixture directly to the affected area and massage it into the skin.

3. Repeat as needed for pain. Store the remaining blend in a cool place out of direct sunlight.

Arthritis Cooling Rub

Makes 12 treatments

4 tablespoons evening primrose oil

24 drops eucalyptus essential oil

24 drops balsam fir essential oil

12 drops spearmint essential oil

1. In a 4-ounce dark amber or cobalt glass bottle, mix the evening primrose oil with the eucalyptus, balsam fir, and spearmint essential oils. Cap the bottle and shake well to combine.
2. Apply 1 teaspoon of this mixture directly to the affected area and massage it into the skin.
3. Store the remaining blend in a cool place out of direct sunlight.

Asthma

Nothing is more frightening than watching your child with asthma struggle to breathe, or to feel the restriction in your own airway. Essential oils can help relieve asthma symptoms through inhalation, especially when activated with heat. An asthma attack can be life threatening, so if using these methods does not improve breathing, use your prescription medications and seek the help of your physician or visit an emergency room, as needed. You can still use the following methods to supplement your doctor's instructions, but restoring breathing is the first priority.

Asthma Steam Relief

Makes 1 treatment

3 cups water

¼ teaspoon (25 drops) eucalyptus essential oil

1. In a small pot over high heat, heat the water until it simmers.
2. Turn off the heat and add the eucalyptus essential oil.

3. Place a trivet or hot pad on a surface you can bend your head over. Place the pot on the trivet. Cover your head with a towel and bend over the steaming water, using the towel to trap the steam. Breathe deeply.
4. Come up for fresh air when you need it, and continue to breathe the steam until the water cools.
5. Do this as often as you like, refreshing the water with new hot water and eucalyptus essential oil.

NOTE: You can substitute lavender or peppermint essential oil for the eucalyptus.

Asthma Vapor Rub

Makes 4 treatments

¼ cup olive oil

12 drops lavender essential oil

8 drops geranium essential oil

2 drops frankincense essential oil

2 drops peppermint essential oil

1. In a 4-ounce dark amber or cobalt glass bottle, combine the olive oil with the lavender, geranium, frankincense, and peppermint essential oils. Cap the bottle and shake well to combine.
2. Rub about 1 tablespoon of the mixture onto the chest. This remedy is particularly effective just before bedtime, so after application, cover up with an old t-shirt or a pajama shirt.
3. Store the remaining blend in a cool place out of direct sunlight.

Back Pain

If you know your back pain comes from the hours you spend standing at work, the new workout you took on a little too enthusiastically, or the way-too-late night you spent at the keyboard, these remedies will help loosen your muscles and take the edge off the pain. If, however, you have a ruptured disk or serious injury, see your doctor before you begin any alternative care plan.

Back Pain Rub

Makes 3 to 4 treatments

2 tablespoons olive oil

10 drops balsam poplar essential oil

10 drops rosemary essential oil

6 drops lavender essential oil

4 drops cassia essential oil

4 drops eucalyptus essential oil

1. In a small glass or metal bowl, mix the olive oil with the balsam poplar, rosemary, lavender, cassia, and eucalyptus essential oils.
2. Rub (or have someone rub) some of the blend into your sore back muscles.
3. Do this twice daily until the pain subsides. Store the remaining blend in a 1-ounce dark amber or cobalt glass bottle in a cool place out of direct sunlight.

Back Pain Soak

Makes 1 treatment

½ cup Epsom salt

10 drops clary sage essential oil

10 drops lavender essential oil

1. In a small glass or metal bowl, use a spoon to combine the Epsom salt with the clary sage and lavender essential oils.
2. Run a warm bath. Add the salt mixture to the water all at once and swish the water around to dissolve the salt.
3. Soak in the tub for 15 to 20 minutes.

Bathroom Care

If the smells of ammonia and chlorine do not appeal to you, several essential oils and odorless baking soda can change the way you clean and disinfect your bathroom.

Bathroom Grout Spray

Makes 16 ounces

2 cups water

2 teaspoons (200 drops) tea tree essential oil

1. In a pint-size glass or metal spray bottle, mix the water and tea tree essential oil. Cap the bottle and shake well to combine.
2. Spritz the mixture on grout or caulking that has mildewed. Don't rinse it—let it work away at the stains. Repeat as needed to defeat mildew and mold.
3. Store the remaining blend in a cool place out of direct sunlight.

Bathtub Cleaner

Makes 1 application

1 cup baking soda

24 drops grapefruit essential oil

24 drops tea tree essential oil

1. In a medium glass or metal bowl, mix the baking soda with the grapefruit and tea tree essential oils.
2. Sprinkle this powder on your tub and scrub it with a sponge or brush.
3. Rinse with water. The waxy soap buildup will rinse away.

Toilet Cleaner

Makes 20 ounces (6 to 10 uses)

2¼ cups water

¼ cup unscented liquid castile soap

4 drops lavender essential oil

4 drops lemon essential oil

4 drops tea tree essential oil

1. In a 32-ounce glass or metal spray bottle, combine the water, castile soap, and the lavender, lemon, and tea tree essential oils. Cap the bottle and shake well to combine.
2. Spray this in your toilet bowl and scrub it with a brush.
3. Flush to rinse. Store the remaining blend in a cool place out of direct sunlight.

Blisters

When fluid is trapped under your skin, it forms a blister, like a bubble on the surface. Blisters can be painful when they burst, and the underlying tissue can become infected. Sometimes these bubbles form as a result of herpes simplex or athlete's foot. Here's how to keep them from becoming more than a nuisance.

Blister Disinfecting Treatment

Makes 5 treatments

10 drops carrier oil of choice

5 drops benzoin (onycha) essential oil

5 drops lavender essential oil

5 drops myrtle essential oil

1. In a small (5-mL) dark amber or cobalt glass bottle, add the carrier oil followed by the benzoin, lavender, and myrtle essential oils. Cap the bottle and shake well to combine.
2. Apply about 5 drops to a cotton swab and gently pat the broken skin, getting the oil under the

broken skin and in contact with the exposed layer.
3. Cover with an adhesive bandage or use a doughnut-shaped moleskin to protect the area if you need to wear shoes.
4. Apply twice daily until the blistered skin closes. Store the remaining blend in a cool place out of direct sunlight.

Blister Interim Care

Makes 1 treatment

1 to 2 drops German chamomile or frankincense essential oil

1. Once the dead skin has lifted naturally away from the blistered spot, carefully trim it off.
2. Treat the new skin underneath with 1 to 2 drops of essential oil daily until it toughens.

Bloating

The mild to severe discomfort of bloating can be a symptom of many things: general indigestion, food allergies or sensitivities, bowel obstruction, or even serious disease. Lemon essential oil acts as a natural diuretic, which can help get things moving again; coriander and peppermint have properties that relieve gas and bloating. If time and the natural remedy provided here do not relieve the situation, seek the help of your physician.

Bloating Relief Rub

Makes 1 treatment

6 drops olive oil

2 drops coriander essential oil

2 drops lemon essential oil

2 drops peppermint essential oil

1. In a small glass or metal bowl, stir together the olive oil with the coriander, lemon, and peppermint essential oils.
2. With your fingertips, apply the blend in a clockwise direction to the abdomen.

3. Lie on your left side for 15 minutes. Breathe in the scents of the essential oils to expand their effectiveness and help you relax.

Body Odor

Body odor comes from bacteria that thrive on the body when you perspire, so people who are more physically active are more likely to produce an odor. You can use body sprays and commercial deodorants to combat this, but essential oils provide a natural option that may be a better fit for your lifestyle.

Deodorant Spray

Makes 3 ounces (5 to 6 applications)

6 tablespoons grain alcohol

30 drops tea tree essential oil

1. In a 4-ounce glass or metal spray bottle, mix the alcohol with the tea tree essential oil. Cap the bottle and shake well to combine.
2. Spray this on your clean armpits after you shower. Store the remaining blend in a cool place out of direct sunlight.

NOTE: For the grain alcohol, I recommend Everclear. In addition to the tea tree essential oil used in this recipe, lavender, lemon, pine, or spearmint essential oils are also antibacterial, and will work well if you prefer one of these scents.

Deodorant Stick

Makes 1 deodorant stick

¼ cup aluminum-free baking soda

¼ cup arrowroot or cornstarch

5 drops of one of the following antibacterial essential oils:

> cumin essential oil
>
> geranium essential oil
>
> lavender essential oil
>
> lemon essential oil
>
> lime essential oil
>
> pine essential oil
>
> spearmint essential oil
>
> thyme essential oil

3 to 5 tablespoons coconut oil

1 empty stick deodorant container

1. In a small glass or metal bowl, mix the baking soda and arrow-root with the essential oil of choice.
2. One tablespoon at a time, add the coconut oil and blend with a pastry blender until fully blended into a paste consistency. Press this into your deodorant container and let stand until the coconut oil solidifies.
3. Apply as needed. Store the remaining blend in a cool place out of direct sunlight.

Deodorant Stick For Hot Climates

Makes 1 deodorant stick

1½ teaspoons grapeseed oil

¾ teaspoon shea butter

¾ teaspoon vegetable glycerin

1 tablespoon baking soda

3 drops cassie essential oil or absolute

3 drops eucalyptus essential oil

3 drops peppermint essential oil

3 drops pine essential oil

3 drops cistus essential oil

1. In a small glass or metal bowl, combine the grapeseed oil, shea butter, and glycerin.
2. Microwave for 10 seconds on high, or until the shea butter melts.
3. Stir in the baking soda and the cassie, eucalyptus, peppermint, pine, and cistus essential oils. Pour the mixture into an empty deodorant container.
4. Refrigerate until it solidifies, and keep refrigerated between uses.

NOTE: This deodorant is especially good for use in warm climates because the shea butter works to combat odor in high heat.

Bronchitis

When the respiratory system becomes inflamed with the respiratory disease known as bronchitis, it produces excess mucus and long spasms of coughing. Bronchitis can worsen and lead to pneumonia, and it can be an indicator of a more serious condition such as chronic obstructive pulmonary disease. Eucalyptus and rosemary are both effective at opening constricted bronchial passages, so direct treatment can be helpful. If your case does not respond to these treatments in one to two days, seek the advice of your physician.

Bronchitis Eucalyptus Diffusion

Makes 1 diffusion

5 drops eucalyptus essential oil

1. To a diffuser, add the eucalyptus essential oil. Take the diffuser into a contained space such as a closed bedroom.
2. Turn on the diffuser and let it run until all the oil has diffused.

Bronchitis Steam Treatment

Makes 1 treatment

3 cups water

¼ teaspoon (25 drops) eucalyptus or rosemary essential oil

1. In a small saucepan over high heat, heat the water to a simmer.
2. Turn off the heat and add the eucalyptus essential oil.
3. Place a trivet or a hot pad on a surface you can bend your head over. Place the pot on the trivet. Cover your head with a towel and bend over the steaming water, using the towel to trap the steam. Breathe deeply.
4. Come up for fresh air when you need it, and continue to breathe the steam until the water cools.
5. Do this as often as you like, refreshing the water with new hot water and essential oil.

Bug Bites and Stings

When mosquitoes bite and the bites become itchy, we want relief as quickly as we can get it. Essential oils with anti-itch properties can solve this problem in minutes, and they can be applied as often as necessary until the bumps disappear. Bee stings are a more serious issue—they can cause pain, fever, and even headaches, and people who are allergic to them can have more dangerous reactions. If the stinger remains in the wound, it can create greater pain and swelling. Check first with a magnifying glass and remove the stinger with tweezers, or by scraping with a credit card. When the stinger is gone, apply an essential oil that has antihistamine and anti-inflammatory properties.

Neat Bug Bite Itch Treatment

Makes 1 treatment

1 drop lavender, peppermint, or wintergreen essential oil

1. Apply 1 drop of the essential oil of choice directly on the sting every 15 minutes for the

first hour after the sting. All 3 oils listed have antipruritic (anti-itch) properties, so they will ease the discomfort of the insect sting.
2. After the first hour, apply 1 drop of any one of these oils 3 times daily until the sting stops bothering you.

Bee Sting Cold Compress

Makes 1 treatment

2 cups cold water

10 drops galbanum essential oil

1 drop chamomile (German or Roman) essential oil

1. In a medium glass or metal bowl or a low basin, mix the water and galbanum essential oil.
2. Soak a hand towel in the water, allowing it to absorb the liquid.
3. Wring out the towel and place it on the bee sting. Wrap it in place using a second hand towel and plastic wrap.
4. If you can, leave this on for several hours (change the compress with a fresh one as it gets warm), and you will defeat the swelling and quell the pain.

5. Once you remove the compress, apply 1 drop of undiluted chamomile essential oil, 3 times a day, directly on the sting location.

Bug Repellent

Here you'll find information for keeping mosquitoes and other biting insects at bay. Citronella is well known as an effective mosquito repellent, and you can buy candles, lamp oil, and a number of other products that dispense it. In the first remedy below, it gets a boost from a number of nature's other effective oils. While few substances are as effective at chasing away mosquitoes as the chemical known as DEET, citronella is also scientifically proven to ward off insects, especially when mixed with pure vanilla extract (the same kind you use in baking—but make sure it's pure vanilla and not imitation). It has a shorter interval of effectiveness than DEET, however, so reapply at least every three hours.

Natural Insect Repellent

Makes 2 or 3 applications

2 tablespoons grain alcohol or rubbing alcohol

12 drops citronella essential oil

12 drops eucalyptus essential oil

6 drops cedarwood essential oil

6 drops geranium essential oil

1. In a small glass or metal bowl, mix the alcohol with the citronella, eucalyptus, cedarwood, and geranium essential oils. Stir to combine well. Transfer to a 2-ounce glass or metal spray bottle.
2. Apply sparingly to your skin, as this is highly concentrated.
3. Use as needed on clothing (except silk, which will be stained on contact) and on the brim of your hat rather than applying all over your skin.
4. Store any remaining repellent in a 1-ounce dark amber or cobalt glass bottle in a cool place out of direct sunlight until you need it again.

NOTE: For the grain alcohol, I recommend Everclear.

Citronella And Vanilla Insect Repellent

Makes 8 ounces

1 cup water

1 tablespoon pure vanilla extract

6 drops lavender essential oil

4 drops lemongrass essential oil

3 drops citronella essential oil

2 drops ginger essential oil

1. In a 12-ounce glass or metal spray bottle, combine the water with the vanilla extract and the lavender, lemongrass, citronella, and ginger essential oils. Cap the bottle and shake well to combine.
2. Spray on your skin and clothing (but not silk, which will be stained on contact), and around the brim of your hat.

Do not spray on your face.

3. Repeat as needed to deter mosquitoes. Store the remaining blend in a cool place out of direct sunlight.

Cellulite

Women tend to have more body fat than men do, and a woman's skin has a thinner outer layer than a man's skin. When the fat packets in women's skin just below the epidermis become enlarged, they become the visible "cottage cheese" skin we know as cellulite. Sadly, no method has been discovered that makes cellulite disappear, but some essential oils can help break it down and make it less visible.

Daily Cellulite Massage

Makes 8 ounces (10 to 14 treatments)

1 cup grapeseed oil

20 drops fennel essential oil

20 drops juniper essential oil

10 drops of one of the following:

    cypress essential oil

    grapefruit essential oil

    lemon essential oil

    rosemary essential oil

    sage essential oil

1. In a small glass or metal bowl, combine the grapeseed oil with the fennel and juniper essential oils, and the essential oil of choice. Mix well.
2. Before you use the massage oil, use a dry body brush (such as a sisal brush) to gently brush the cellulite-stricken areas of your body until your skin is pink.
3. Daily, massage the oil into your cellulite areas for 10 minutes to diminish its appearance.
4. Store the remaining mixture in a dark amber or cobalt glass bottle or jar in a cool place out of direct sunlight.

Cellulite Helichrysum Treatment

Makes 1 treatment

1 tablespoon olive oil

5 drops helichrysum essential oil

1. In a small glass or metal bowl, mix the olive oil and helichrysum essential oil.
2. Daily, massage this blend into your problem cellulite areas until it is absorbed into your skin and you see results.

NOTE: Helichrysum essential oil is a natural anti-inflammatory, making it effective for a wide range of skin issues. If you're not seeing the results you want from your daily massage (and you've already taken off some weight and you're getting regular exercise), try adding this to your daily regimen.

Chapped Lips

Whether you live in a climate with six months of bitter winter or in the bone-dry desert, you know what discomfort chapped lips can create. These simple remedies give you moisturizing relief along with the regenerative powers of essential oils. Which one you use is entirely a matter of personal preference; some people prefer the clear, shiny aloe vera gel on their lips, while others like the richness of shea butter.

Chapped Lips Gel

Makes 1 treatment

1 large drop aloe vera gel

1 drop frankincense or myrrh essential oil

1. Place 1 drop of aloe vera gel on your index finger.
2. Add 1 drop of your essential oil of choice.
3. Smooth between your finger and thumb to mix.
4. Apply to your lips. Repeat as often as you like to fight dryness and chapping.

Shea Butter For Chapped Lips

Makes 1 treatment

1 fingertip's worth of shea butter (about ¼ teaspoon)

1 drop cistus essential oil

1. Place the shea butter on your index finger.
2. Add 1 drop of cistus essential oil.
3. Smooth between your finger and thumb to mix.
4. Apply to your lips. Repeat as often as you like to fight dryness and chapping.

NOTE: If you don't have cistus essential oil, lavender, myrrh, or frankincense essential oil will work.

Chilblains

If you've been exposed to cold, damp conditions for long periods, you may know the discomfort of chilblains—also known as pernio. The small, swollen, itchy spots on fingers, toes, ears, and nose are not life threatening, but they can be a nuisance.

Chilblains Layering Treatment

Makes 1 treatment

1 drop myrrh essential oil

1 drop lavender essential oil

1 drop helichrysum essential oil

3 drops sweet almond oil

1. Using your fingertips, apply the myrrh essential oil to the affected area.
2. Next, apply the lavender essential oil on top of the myrrh.
3. Now apply the helichrysum essential oil over the lavender.
4. Top these with the sweet almond oil.
5. Repeat this up to 4 times daily until the chilblains are healed.

Soothing Sandalwood And Cedarwood Bath For Chilblains

Makes 5 treatments

5 tablespoons calendula oil

6 drops cedarwood essential oil

6 drops lavender essential oil

6 drops sandalwood essential oil

1. In a 4-ounce dark amber or cobalt glass bottle, combine the calendula oil with the cedarwood, lavender, and sandalwood essential oils. Cap the bottle and shake well to combine.
2. Run a warm bath and, while the water is running, add 1 tablespoon of the blend to the warm water.
3. Soak for at least 15 minutes.
4. Repeat daily until the chilblains are healed.
5. Store the remaining bath oil in a cool place out of direct sunlight.

Colds and Flu

Sneezing, sniffles, upper respiratory congestion, coughing, and low-grade fever are all common symptoms of the world's most ubiquitous and contagious malady. There's no cure for the common cold and no easy way to fight the flu, but you can arm yourself against the next onslaught by keeping some antiviral and symptom-fighting essential oils on hand, including eucalyptus, fir, frankincense, lavender, lemon, myrrh, myrtle, spearmint, and tea tree.

Cold- And Flu-Fighting Steam

Makes 1 treatment

1 to 1½ cups steaming-hot water

1 drop balsam fir essential oil

1 drop lavender essential oil

1 drop myrrh essential oil

1 drop tea tree essential oil

1. Into a medium glass or metal bowl set on a heatproof surface, pour the hot water.

2. Add the balsam fir, lavender, myrrh, and tea tree essential oils.
3. Place a trivet or hot pad on a surface you can bend your head over. Place the bowl on the trivet. Cover your head with a towel and bend over the steaming water, using the towel to trap the steam. Breathe deeply.
4. Come up for fresh air when you need it, and continue to breathe the steam until the water cools.
5. Repeat this process as often as you wish.

Vapor Rub For Colds And Flu

Makes 5 treatments

2 tablespoons sweet almond oil or jojoba oil

15 drops rosemary essential oil

10 drops eucalyptus essential oil

5 drops lemon essential oil

1. In a 2-ounce dark amber or cobalt glass bottle, combine the sweet almond oil with the rosemary, eucalyptus, and lemon essential oils.

2. Gently rub this blend on your chest, neck, cheekbones, and around your nose, following the line of your sinus cavities.
3. Repeat 2 to 3 times daily until your symptoms clear. Store the remaining blend in a cool place out of direct sunlight.

Colic

When your baby cries uncontrollably for hours at a time, and continues to cry like this more than three days a week for several weeks in a row, she has colic—and you have sleepless nights and high stress levels. The condition is not permanent, but no parent can bear to hear their baby cry without doing something to soothe her.

Colic Massage

Makes 1 treatment

1 teaspoon sweet almond oil

1 drop geranium essential oil

1 drop lavender essential oil

1. In your palm, mix the sweet almond oil with the geranium and lavender essential oils until they are warm.
2. Using a little of the oil on your fingertips, gently rub this blend in a circular, clockwise motion on your baby's stomach.

3. When the baby becomes quieter, turn him over onto his stomach and continue the gentle massage on his back.

Colic Warm Compress

Makes 1 compress

2 cups warm water

1 drop lavender essential oil

1. In a small glass or metal bowl, combine the water and lavender essential oil.
2. Place a washcloth on the surface of the water and let it become saturated.
3. Lift the washcloth from the water and wring out the excess water.
4. As your baby lies on her back, place the wet compress on her stomach. Once the compress cools to the point it no longer keeps your baby warm and comfortable, remove it.
5. If the crying begins again, repeat the process.

Conjunctivitis

Conjunctivitis, or "pink eye," is an infection of the transparent membrane covering the white part of the eye. Not only is it irritating, it's also highly contagious, and children often pass it from one to the next. You can take steps to relieve the itching and soreness using warm compresses and rose essential oil, but anything you use must be disinfected immediately to keep from spreading the infection to others in the family.

Conjunctivitis Compress

Makes 1 compress

2 cups warm water

5 drops rose essential oil

1. In a small glass or metal bowl, combine the water and rose essential oil.
2. Place a washcloth on the surface of the water and let it become saturated.
3. Lift the washcloth from the water and wring out the excess water.

4. Place the wet compress over the affected eye. (It may be easiest to have your child lie down for this, or for you to lie down if you're the one affected.)
5. When the compress cools to the point it no longer feels warm, remove it. Immediately wash out the compress with soap and hot water, and wash your hands, as well.
6. Repeat as often as you wish. If the condition doesn't clear up in 2 to 3 days, see your doctor. The infection may be bacterial rather than viral, and antibiotics may be required.

Cough

Colds, allergies, and post-nasal drip can create a nagging tickle that just doesn't seem to go away. Cough drops made with honey or horehound can be effective natural remedies. While no essential oil should be taken internally, you can soothe the cough using your vaporizer and a range of essential oils—and throat and chest rubs can penetrate to help clear the source of the tickle.

Chest Rub For Cough

Makes 5 treatments

2 tablespoons olive oil

15 drops eucalyptus essential oil

10 drops balsam fir essential oil

1. In a 2-ounce dark amber or cobalt glass bottle or jar, combine the olive oil with the eucalyptus and balsam fir essential oils.
2. Rub this blend over your chest and throat.
3. Repeat as desired. Store the remaining blend in a cool place out of direct sunlight.

Cough Congestion-Busting Vapor

Makes 1 treatment

3 drops each of 1 or more of the following:

    chamomile essential oil (German or Roman)

    frankincense essential oil

    ginger essential oil

    lavender essential oil

    oregano essential oil

    sandalwood essential oil

    tea tree essential oil

1. To the water in your vaporizer, add the essential oils of choice, and turn it on.
2. Stay in the room with the vaporizer running for at least 15 minutes every hour.
3. Repeat as often as you wish.

Cradle Cap

It looks potentially worrisome to new parents, but cradle cap is a very common ailment that children grow out of after the age of one. The crust of dead skin cells can be remedied with a simple balm that kills bacteria when gently massaged into your baby's scalp.

Cradle Cap Scalp Treatment

Makes 1 treatment

1 teaspoon jojoba oil

2 drops geranium or rose geranium essential oil

1. In your palm, combine the jojoba oil with the geranium essential oil. Rub both palms together to warm the oils.
2. Gently apply the blend to your baby's scalp. Be careful not to get any of the oil in his eyes.
3. With a baby brush, gently rub the oil into the affected area.
4. Repeat this 3 times daily until the condition clears.

Cuts and Scrapes

Use the antiseptic and antibacterial qualities of essential oils in place of commercial first-aid creams for minor cuts and scrapes. Many essential oils can prevent infection and allow your wound to heal naturally and effectively, without the sting of an alcohol-based disinfectant.

Wash For Minor Cuts

Makes 1 treatment

Warm water

3 drops of one of the following:

> eucalyptus essential oil
>
> lavender essential oil
>
> lemon essential oil
>
> pine essential oil
>
> sandalwood essential oil
>
> spikenard essential oil
>
> tea tree essential oil

1. Fill a sink or large glass or metal bowl with warm water.
2. Add 3 drops of the essential oil of choice.
3. Bathe the cut or scrape in the water, then dry with a clean towel.

Neat Treatment For Cuts And Scrapes

Makes 1 treatment

1 or 2 drops of one of the following antibacterial essential oils:

    eucalyptus essential oil

    lavender essential oil

    lemon essential oil

    pine essential oil

    sandalwood essential oil

    spikenard essential oil

    tea tree essential oil

1. Place 1 or 2 drops of the essential oil of choice directly on the cut or scrape.
2. If there is a chance the wound could pick up dirt or could be reinjured, use sterile materials to bandage the cut or scrape.

3. Change the bandage daily, and reapply the essential oil, neat, with each new bandage.

NOTE: Eucalyptus, lavender, and tea tree essential oils are all soothing, as well as good shields against infection.

Diaper Rash

If you don't like the idea of using commercial diaper rash products on your baby's sensitive skin, essential oils provide an alternative. Here are options that will cool the rash and bring comfort to your baby.

Soothing Diaper Rash Wash

Makes 20 treatments

10 drops lavender essential oil

10 drops yarrow essential oil

2 cups warm water

1. In a small (5-mL) dark amber or cobalt glass bottle, blend the lavender and yarrow essential oils. Cap the bottle and shake well to combine.
2. In a medium glass or metal bowl, combine the water with 1 drop of the lavender-yarrow essential oil blend.
3. Soak a soft cloth in the warm water, wring it out, and use it to cleanse your baby.
4. Dry the diaper area and use a cotton ball to apply additional oil-treated water to your baby's bottom.

5. Store the remaining oil blend in a cool place out of direct sunlight until needed.

Diaper Rash Protection

Makes 20 treatments

10 drops lavender essential oil

10 drops yarrow essential oil

4 teaspoons sweet almond oil or jojoba oil

1. In a small (5-mL) dark amber or cobalt glass bottle, blend the lavender and yarrow essential oils. Cap the bottle and shake well to combine.
2. In your palm, mix the sweet almond oil with 1 drop of the lavender-yarrow essential oil blend.
3. Smooth a light layer of this protective oil over the diaper area before putting on a new diaper.
4. Store the remaining blend in a cool place out of direct sunlight until needed.

Diarrhea

The clinical definition of diarrhea includes watery bowel movements of abnormal frequency—say, every hour or so for several hours or longer. An intestinal disorder of this kind can make you pass a quart of liquid in a day, so drinking lots of water (or sports drinks that supply the electrolyte balance you need) is the most important thing you can do. Diarrhea that lasts two days or more becomes a health risk because of the danger of dehydration. If you frequently experience loose stools that you can't connect to a stomach virus or food poisoning, you may have a chronic condition that requires medical intervention. If your diarrhea does not begin to clear up after four days, consult your doctor.

Antibacterial Massage For Diarrhea

Makes 3 treatments

1 tablespoon olive oil

9 drops lavender essential oil

3 drops cedarwood essential oil

3 drops eucalyptus essential oil

3 drops tea tree essential oil

1. In a 1-ounce dark amber or cobalt glass bottle, combine the olive oil with the lavender, cedarwood, eucalyptus, and tea tree essential oils. Cap the bottle and shake well to combine.
2. Apply 1 teaspoon to your abdomen, massaging it in a circular, clockwise motion until the oils are absorbed.
3. Repeat as needed after each episode of diarrhea. Store the remaining blend in a cool place out of direct sunlight.

Ear Infection

Not every earache is an infection. Some come from a buildup of fluid in the ear, which becomes painful when the pressure increases during a cold or when seasonal allergies flare up. When pain persists even when the sinus congestion has cleared, there may be an infection present, and if the pain continues for more than a few hours, it's time to have a doctor take a look inside. Ear infections can cause long-term complications, especially in children. If you have a baby or toddler who keeps holding or pulling on one ear and you can see redness inside, call your doctor.

Ear Infection Olive Oil Remedy

Makes 4 treatments

1 tablespoon warm olive oil

2 drops cedarwood essential oil

2 drops lavender essential oil

2 drops Roman chamomile essential oil

2 drops rosemary essential oil

1. In a 1-ounce dark amber or cobalt glass bottle, mix the olive oil with the cedarwood, lavender, Roman chamomile, and rosemary essential oils. Cap the bottle and shake well to combine.
2. With a cotton swab, apply the oil around the opening of the ear, around the outside of the ear, and on the earlobe.
3. Place a warm compress (such as a folded washcloth soaked in warm water and wrung nearly dry) over the affected ear to warm the oils and help them penetrate.
4. Repeat every 2 hours until the pressure subsides. If the pain continues for more than 6 hours, consult a doctor.
5. Store the remaining blend in a cool place out of direct sunlight.

Ear Infection Cotton Remedy

Makes 1 treatment

3 drops lavender essential oil

1. Place the lavender essential oil on a cotton ball, and place this over the ear opening.
2. Leave it in place overnight.

Eczema

Eczema presents as red, itchy, peeling patches of skin that arise in a multitude of situations, from using a new soap or detergent to enduring a period of prolonged stress. When you find yourself scratching where you usually don't scratch, reach for your essential oils to calm the inflammation.

Eczema Anti-Itch Blend

Makes 3 to 5 treatments

1 tablespoon coconut oil

2 drops frankincense essential oil

2 drops helichrysum essential oil

1 drop geranium essential oil

1 drop thyme essential oil

1. In a small glass or metal bowl, mix the coconut oil with the frankincense, helichrysum, geranium, and thyme essential oils.
2. With your fingers, apply this blend to the itchy areas.

3. Cover the treated area with gauze. If the area is on your hand or foot, put on white cotton gloves or cotton socks. Keep the area covered throughout the day. If you must remove the gauze or gloves, reapply the treatment, up to 3 times per day.
4. Repeat as needed until the itching stops.
5. Store any unused blend in a small (5-mL) dark amber or cobalt glass bottle in a cool place out of direct sunlight.

Fatigue

If you prefer to battle that 3 p.m. drowsiness with a natural remedy instead of an energy drink, your essential oils can help. The best cure for fatigue is sleep, of course, but that's not practical in the middle of the workday or if your evening is loaded with your children's activities. Here are some remedies to help you keep moving when your eyelids have other ideas.

Fatigue-Fighting Diffusion

Makes 4 diffusions

4 drops anise essential oil

4 drops cassia essential oil

3 drops cinnamon essential oil

3 drops pine essential oil

2 drops bdellium essential oil

1. In a small (5-mL) dark amber or cobalt glass bottle, mix the anise, cassia, cinnamon, pine, and bdellium essential oils. Cap the bottle and shake well to combine.

2. Add 4 drops of this blend to your diffuser, and run the diffuser for 15 minutes in your car or office (if you have one with a door), or at home.
3. Cap the jar tightly and store any remaining oil blend in a cool place out of direct sunlight.

Stimulating Air Freshener

Makes 10 applications

3 tablespoons distilled water or spring water

3 tablespoons vodka or grain alcohol

12 drops peppermint essential oil

12 drops lemon essential oil

6 drops frankincense essential oil

1. In a 4-ounce glass or metal spray bottle, mix the water and vodka with the peppermint, lemon, and frankincense essential oils. Cap the bottle and shake well to combine.
2. Spray this in your room or car once every 2 hours, as needed. Store the remaining blend in a cool place out of direct sunlight.

NOTE: Any brand of vodka will do but for the grain alcohol, I recommend Everclear.

Fever

The symptoms caused by fever can make you miserable: dizziness, lack of appetite, alternating chills and sweating, fatigue, and muscle aches. A number of essential oils (any of the mint oils, as well as bay and cassia) can help reduce a fever through their overall cooling effects. If the ill person is a child, review the precautions of the following recipe before treating young children.

Fever-Cooling Neat Treatment

Makes 1 treatment

3 or 4 drops peppermint essential oil

1. Place the peppermint essential oil on a cotton ball.
2. Apply the oil directly to the back of the neck and the soles of the feet.
3. Repeat this every 30 minutes until the fever goes down.

CAUTIONARY NOTE: Peppermint essential oil should not be used with children under 7 years of age.

If your child is 7 or older, it will need to be diluted. Dilute 1 or 2 drops of peppermint essential oil in 1 tablespoon of a carrier oil of your choice before applying it to your child's skin.

Fever-Reducing Cold Pack

Makes 1 treatment

1 cup cold water

3 drops spearmint essential oil

1 drop eucalyptus essential oil

1. In a small glass or metal bowl, mix the water with the spearmint and eucalyptus essential oils.
2. Place a hand towel or a cloth bandage on the surface of the water and let it become saturated.
3. Remove the towel and wring out any excess water.
4. Place the cold compress on the forehead. Cover it with a plastic bag or sheet of plastic wrap to contain the moisture. Hold the compress and plastic in place with a hand towel, or tie it in place with an elastic bandage, just tight enough to hold the compress.

5. When the compress warms to body temperature, replace it with another cold compress. Repeat until the fever is reduced.

Flatulence

If you feel bloated, crampy, and generally uncomfortable and you feel like you're expelling a lot of gas, you are not alone. Most people produce up to three pints of it a day, and pass gas about 14 times a day, according to colon-rectal.com. This doesn't make it socially acceptable, however, and the discomfort makes it even less pleasant. The number-one remedy for flatulence in the entire essential oils apothecary is peppermint. In addition to the following remedy, you can get peppermint hard candy or other edible drops at any convenience store or drug store.

Flatulence Peppermint Rub

Makes 1 treatment

4 to 6 drops peppermint essential oil

1. Place the peppermint essential oil in your palm and rub your hands together.
2. Then, rub your palms over your stomach and around your navel in a clockwise direction. The oil will be absorbed through your skin and will help relieve indigestion and flatulence.

Eucalyptus For Respiratory Issues

Do you have breathing issues? If the answer is yes, then let's take a look at eucalyptus. This is an essential oil that is great for any homemade cleaning, since it can be used to help diffuse the air to make it cleaner. Also, it is an expectorant, which is another benefit of this. May essential oils can be used to help clear out the sinuses, and this is no exception.

Ideally, the best way to use this is to use about 10 drops of this oil, 2 tablespoons of dish soap, and some water to your mop as you clean up the floors in your house. If you have a cold or respiratory infection, use a few drops with some coconut oil and then rub it into your chest to help with the breathing issues. This is also used in a diffuser for best results, since it can help freshen up the air in your home. Eucalyptus smells great too, and while it is pretty strong and might not be for everyone, this is a great one if you're looking to help clear out your sinuses and help with breathing.

Frankincense for the Immune System

Frankincense is probably the ultimate immune system booster, but it also can help with beautification and lowering the presence of scars. It can be used as well to help reduce the feeling of pain, and it can create a better sort of relief.

Now, one thing of note, is that this is one of the pricier oils, but it's pricier for a good reason. It's actually pricy because of how much it can actually help you, and most people swear by this one and lavender as the ultimate in essential oils. You can relieve the tension headaches that might come up with it, and you can create a very relaxing bath with this, combined with lavender. You can also use this topically to help with the appearance of blemishes and scars.

If you have a cut, put a drop of it onto there to help relieve the pain that you're in. the same thing goes for bites and stings that you have, since it'll reduce the itching that is there.

The best way to use this is to combine this with lavender, since it can create the ultimate stress reliever, and it can help take out the pain from tension reaches. Using two drops of each together can help with this.

If you're going to use this to help reduce the appearance of scars, then use a couple of drops near the area each day. It does take a little bit, but it does help with the appearance of them, since often this can be quite unseemly.

However, did you know that this can also help with the emotions many of us suffer from? If you have menstrual issues, such as PMS, or even emotional issues and anxiety, rubbing a little bit of this onto the face, or even using this as a diffuser, can ultimately help you with some of the pain you're going through. You can use this to help relieve the mental tensions, and overall, it can make a big difference in the future of your health and wellness.

This is a good one that you can use all over on the body, and it definitely can make a huge difference in your overall personal wellness as well.

Peppermint for the Respiratory and Digestive Systems

Along with lavender, peppermint is probably one of the best essential oils out here, for it showcases the benefits of the oil to the respiratory as well. However, it takes it a step further, helping with the digestive system in turn as well. How though? Well, it actually is a very powerful antioxidant, and it is one of the few oils that you can ingest without having to do too much dilution. It can also be used to help with nausea, headaches, and even energy output. It can be used topically in order to help relieve pain, just make sure you don't get it into your eyes. If you want to use a cooling spritz that can help you keep cool and rejuvenate the body, then this one is for you. just putting about 5 drops in a spray bottle made of glass can really help.

If you're suffering from nausea from either morning sickness or the flu, grab the bottle, open it, and inhale it deeply. Do make sure that you take a nice, deep breath, and this can help with that.

This is the essential oil for the respiratory and digestive system, and this as well shows the powerful benefits of essential oils, and it is one of the key oils that will help you with improving your life, your breathing, and also your overall wellness.

Tea Tree Oil for bites

Bug bites are never fun, and it can be quite hard for a person that has them. They can sting, and the problem with many of them is that it can be a problem to treat, since ultimately, you might be throwing more chemicals into there than you care to admit. However, tea tree oil is a natural means to help you get the sting out of there, but it's also an oil that's actually a must for almost all homes. Why is that?

Well, it actually is a very powerful antibacterial period, meaning it can be used in the home not only as a cleaner, but it also can be used every time you get hurt. Putting it on the skin will help to fight off the infection, but as well soothe the skin, since often it can be quite painful. For burns, this is a natural slave, and it can be used to help alleviate the pain from this.

Now, if you want to help clean up the body and such, you can put this into a homemade shampoo to help bring life to your hair. If you have any sorts of rashes from whatever it might be, put it directly onto the skin to help with reducing the itching that might be there. If you want to clean up your home, you can add a few drops of this to a cleaning spray that is natural to help kill off the various germs that might be there. It also can be put directly onto surfaces to help directly kill germs, and it's natural too so it helps.

It also can be used topically to help reduce any sorts of blemishes on the skin, especially acne and other infections. It also can be put on a wart to help reduce the size of it, and if you have lice, mix it with a shampoo to help reduce the appearance of it.

This is a good one for pretty much any ouchie, and that's one of the huge benefits to essential oils. Once you know how to use it, which is typically a simple topical application, you can certainly get the most out of this, and you'll be able to reap this benefit when you do decide to use this product.

More Recipes

Altitude Sickness

Oral—Take a capsule filled with 5 drops of lemon, and 2 drops each of frankincense, cedarwood, and peppermint 1 to 3 times daily.

Alzheimer's Disease/Dementia

Topical—Massage 6 to 8 drops of lavender to the shoulders, back, and bottoms of the feet to improve sleep quality. Apply 1 to 2 drops each of frankincense, vetiver, and rosemary to the base of the neck, crown of the head, and behind the ears, 2 to 4 times daily. Apply 8 to 10 drops of orange oil on the bottoms of the feet, 1 to 2 times daily.

Inhalation—Apply 1 drop each of rosemary and peppermint oil on palms, rub together, and cup over nose and mouth to inhale as often as needed. Alternately, place 2 to 3 drops each of rosemary and peppermint oil in boiling water and place next to individual to inhale.

Amoebic Dysentery

Oral—Take a capsule filled with 3 drops each of oregano and lemongrass and 1 drop of thyme, 1 to 3 times daily.

Topical—Apply 1 drop each of basil, fennel, copaiba and thyme to the lower abdomen, 2 to 4 times daily.

Anemia

Oral—Take one or a combination of 4 to 6 drops of German chamomile, lemon, frankincense, or helichrysum, 2 times daily.

Topical—Apply 1 to 3 drops of German chamomile, frankincense, lemon, and/or helichrysum to the bottom of the feet, 2 to 4 times daily.

Aneurysm

Topical—Mix 5 drops cistus and 1 drop each of helichrysum and cypress in equal parts carrier oil and apply to the head and back of the neck, every 2 hours.

Oral—Take 10 drops of lemon, 3 to 4 times daily.

Anger

Inhalation—Place 1 drop each of ylang ylang, orange, and German chamomile on a tissue and inhale as needed.

Topical—Massage the soles of the feet (focusing on the liver area on the outside of the right foot) with 1 drop each of ylang ylang, orange, German chamomile, and lavender, 1 to 3 times daily.

Angina

Topical—Apply 1 to 3 drops each of wintergreen, clove, goldenrod, ylang ylang, and/or helichrysum over heart area, 2 to 4 times daily.

Oral—Take 10 drops of a combination of helichrysum, clove, lemon, or orange, 1 to 3 times daily.

Ankylosing Spondylitis

Oral—Take a capsule filled with 7 drops of frankincense and 3 drops each of balsam fir and copaiba, 2 to 4 times daily. Take a capsule filled with 15 drops of lemon once daily.

Topical—Apply 2 drops each of basil, balsam fir, cypress, copaiba, and lavender to the back and hips, 1 to 3 times daily. Apply 3 to 5 drops of oregano, thyme, basil, cypress, wintergreen, marjoram, and peppermint (layered in that order, 1 at a time) to the spine and massage into back on either side of the spine, 2 times weekly.

Other—Keep the back limber by performing yoga cat-cow poses for 1 to 2 minutes immediately before bedtime.

Anxiety

Topical—Apply 1 to 3 drops of lavender and cedarwood to the base of the skull, neck, and head.

Oral—Take 1 capsule filled with 3 drops each of lavender, cedarwood, and German chamomile, 1 to 3 times daily.

Inhalation—Apply 1 to 2 drops of cedarwood and lavender to 1 palm, rub together with the other palm, and cup hands over mouth and nose to inhale as often as needed.

Apnea, Sleep

Topical—Apply 1 to 3 drops of thyme and/or black spruce to the bottoms of each big toe and the feet before retiring to bed.

Inhalation—Apply 1 drop each of black spruce and balsam fir on pillowcase before bedtime.

Appendicitis

Severe abdominal pain requires medical attention. The appendix could burst if not treated in a timely manner, which allows its contents to leak out and spreads infection throughout your abdomen.

Oral—Take a capsule filed with 3 drops each of ginger, lemon, and peppermint, and 2 drops each of basil and oregano, 2 to 4 times daily.

Topical—Apply 2 drops each of wintergreen, orange, and lemon to the arch of the right foot and near the heel.

Other—**DO NOT** massage the abdomen. Appendicitis is considered a medical emergency and professional care should be sought as soon as possible.

Arachnoid Cysts

Topical—Apply 3 drops each of frankincense, vetiver, sandalwood, and blue spruce along the entire spine and to the base of the hairline. Apply 8 to 10 drops of orange oil to the feet, 2 times daily. Apply 3 to 5 drops of oregano, thyme, basil, cypress, wintergreen, marjoram, and peppermint (layered in that order, 1 at a time) to the spine and massage into back on either side of the spine, 2 times weekly.

Oral—Take a capsule filled with 5 drops each of frankincense, vetiver, and sandalwood, 2 to 4 times daily.

Arthritis (Rheumatoid)

Topical—Apply 1 to 2 drops each of peppermint, wintergreen, frankincense, eucalyptus, and copaiba to affected area as needed (cypress and helichrysum may also be added to increase circulation to affected joints). Apply 3 to 5 drops of oregano and clove to the bottom of the feet, 2 times daily.

Oral—Take 1 capsule filled with 4 drops each of frankincense, balsam fir, and copaiba, and 1 drop of nutmeg, 2 times daily.

Arthrogryposis Multiplex Congenita (Arthrogryposis)

Topical—Create a mixture of 1 drop each of marjoram, cypress, frankincense, lavender, basil, and German chamomile in 4 teaspoons of carrier oil and massage into the affected joints/muscles up to 3 times daily.

Asperger Syndrome

Topical—Apply 1 to 3 drops of blue spruce to both sides of the neck, 1 to 3 times daily. Apply 8 to 10 drops of orange oil to the bottoms of the feet, 1 to 2 times daily. Apply 2 drops each of frankincense, vetiver, and sandalwood to the forehead and behind the ears 1 to 3 times daily. Applying a mixture of 2 drops each of lavender, ylang ylang, blue tansy, and orange to the bottoms of the feet or by gently stroking the person's head with the oils on your hand may be calming during hyperactive episodes.

Inhalation—Inhaling 1 to 2 drops of lavender may reduce anxious feelings.

Other—Many individuals with Asperger syndrome are opposed to touch and certain odors, so it may be necessary to offer them the recommended oils and allow them to choose which ones to apply.

Asthma

Topical—Apply 1 to 2 drops each of ginger, myrtle, thyme, and pine to the chest as often as needed. Apply 1 to 2 drops of oregano, peppermint, thyme, and myrtle to the bottoms of the feet, 2 to 3 times daily.

Inhalation—Apply 1 to 2 drops of lavender, ginger, or myrtle to 1 palm, rub together with other palm, cup over mouth and nose and inhale. Place 4 to 6 drops each of 1 or more of myrtle, ginger or lavender in 3 inches of hot water that is not too hot to touch with your hand and cover head with towel to inhale every 4 to 6 hours.

Atherosclerosis

Oral—Ingest 4 drops each of rosemary, juniper, lemon, and ylang ylang, 2 to 4 times daily.

Topical—Apply ylang ylang, rosemary, and/or juniper on carotid arteries and over heart, 2 to 4 times daily.

Athlete's Foot

Topical—Soak foot in Epsom salts (use coarse sea salt for diabetics) bath with melaleuca (tea tree) and lavender added directly to the salts (not the water), 2 times daily. Apply 3 to 5 drops each of oregano, lemongrass, and melaleuca (tea tree) to affected areas after soaking.

ATTENTION-DEFICIT DISORDER (ADD) Or ATTENTION-DEFICIT HYPERACTIVITY DISORDER (ADHD)

Topical—Apply 1 to 3 drops each of cedarwood, German chamomile, and lavender and/or frankincense and vetiver to the back of the neck, brain stem, and head up to 8 times daily (frankincense and vetiver increase focus, lavender and German chamomile help calm anxious feelings). Apply 3 to 5 drops of orange, 2 to 3 times daily.

Oral—Take 1 capsule filled with 2 drops each of cedarwood, lavender, and frankincense, 2 times daily.

Autism

Topical—Apply 1 drop of blue spruce to both sides of the neck, 1 to 3 times daily. Apply 8 to 10 drops of orange oil to the bottoms of the feet, 1 to 2 times daily. Apply 2 drops each of frankincense, vetiver, and sandalwood to the forehead and behind the ears, 1 to 3 times daily. Applying a mixture of 2 drops each of lavender, ylang ylang, blue tansy, and orange to the bottoms of the feet or by gently stroking the person's head with the oils on your hand may be calming during hyperactive episodes.

Inhalation—Inhaling 1 to 2 drops of lavender may reduce anxious feelings.

Other—Many individuals with autism are opposed to touch and certain odors, so it may be necessary to offer them the recommended oils and allow them to choose which ones to apply.

Autoimmune Disorder (Immune Balancing Protocol)

Oral—Take a capsule filled with 3 drops each of vetiver, frankincense, lavender and spruce, and 1 drop of clove, morning and evening. Take an additional capsule with 3 drops each of clove, oregano, lemon, cinnamon, and 1 drop of eucalyptus and melaleuca (tea tree) once midday.

Back Pain

Topical—Apply a combination of 1 to 3 drops of wintergreen, black spruce, balsam fir, copaiba, peppermint, and frankincense to affected area, 2 to 4 times daily. For muscular back pain, use 2 to 3 drops of basil and marjoram instead.

Oral—Take 1 capsule with 5 drops each of frankincense, copaiba, and balsam fir, 2 times daily.

Barrett's Esophagus

Oral—Swallow 5 drops each of lemon and ginger in water, 2 to 4 times daily.

Topical—Apply 2 drops each of frankincense, ginger, lavender, and blue tansy externally to the throat and breastbone areas, 2 to 4 times daily.

Basal Cell Carcinoma

Topical—Apply 2 to 4 drops each of sandalwood, frankincense, geranium, cinnamon, and cypress to the affected area, 3 to 5 times daily. Apply 8 to 10 drops of orange oil to the bottoms of the feet, 2 to 3 times daily. Apply more geranium and helichrysum as the area begins to heal to prevent scarring.

Oral—Take 0.018 to 0.045 ml of enriched frankincense or frankincense per pound of body weight (for example, a 150-pound person would take 2.7 to 6.75 ml daily) in 3 to 6 divided doses throughout the day with food for 21 days.

Bed Wetting (Nocturnal Urination)

Topical—Apply 3 to 5 drops of cypress mixed with carrier oil over the stomach and bladder area before going to bed.

Bell's Palsy

Topical—Apply 1 drop each of frankincense, helichrysum, geranium, blue spruce, and copaiba directly behind and underneath both ears and on the affected area of the face, 2 to 3 times daily. Apply 3 to 5 drops of oregano, thyme, basil, cypress, wintergreen, marjoram, and peppermint (layered in that order, 1 at a time) to the spine and massage into back on either side of the spine, 2 times weekly.

Oral—Take 1 capsule filled with 2 drops each of clove, oregano, lemon, cinnamon, and 1 drop of eucalyptus, 2 to 3 times daily.

Benign Motor Neuron Disorder

Topical—Apply 3 to 5 drops of oregano, thyme, basil, cypress, wintergreen, marjoram, and peppermint (layered in that order, 1 at a time) to the spine and massage into back on either side of the spine, 2 to 4 times weekly; apply 1 drop each of blue spruce, vetiver, frankincense, and sandalwood behind the ears and at the base of the skull, 2 to 4 times daily. Apply 10 drops of orange oil on the bottoms of the feet, 2 times daily. Apply 1 to 2 drops each of marjoram, pine, lavender, and lemongrass to the major muscles, 1 to 3 times daily.

Oral—Take a capsule filled with 5 drops each of frankincense, sandalwood, and myrrh, 1 to 3 times daily.

Benign Prostatic Hyperplasia (Bph), Enlarged Prostate

Topical—Apply 1 drop of frankincense, myrrh, orange, balsam fir, and copaiba heavily diluted to the area between the anus and scrotum, 2 times daily.

Retention—Mix 3 drops each of frankincense, myrrh, and tsuga in 1 tablespoon of vegetable oil and insert rectally. Retain as long as possible.

Oral—Take a capsule filled with 4 drops each of oregano, vetiver, and rosemary, 1 to 3 times daily.

Bipolar Disorder

Only use in conjunction with Western medical options and with approval from a physician.

Topical—Apply 1 drop each of frankincense, cedarwood, sandalwood, spruce, and lavender to the base of the skull and behind the ears, 2 to 4 times daily. Apply 2 to 3 drops of helichrysum over the liver, 1 to 3 times daily. Apply 5 drops of orange and 2 drops of lemon to the bottoms of the feet, 3 times daily.

Oral—Take a capsule filled with 5 drops of helichrysum, 1 to 3 times daily.

Bites (Animal)

Topical—Apply 1 drop each of thyme, oregano, lavender, German chamomile, and lemongrass every 15 minutes for the first 2 hours, and then 1 time per hour for the next 24 to 48 hours. Apply peppermint to the bite as needed for pain.

Oral—Take a capsule filled with 3 drops of oregano, and 1 drop each of eucalyptus, melaleuca (tea tree), and thyme, 2 to 3 times daily.

Bladder Infection

Oral—Take 1 capsule filled with 2 drops each of clove, oregano, lemon, cinnamon, and 1 drop of eucalyptus, 2 to 3 times daily.

Topical—Apply 2 drops each of clove, oregano, eucalyptus, and cinnamon to the bottoms of the feet, 2 to 3 times daily. Apply 3 drops each of juniper, oregano, and frankincense with 10 drops of vegetable oil to the pelvic area, 1 to 3 times daily.

Other—Drink 2 8-ounce glasses of unsweetened cranberry or blueberry juice daily for 3 to 5 days.

Bleeding

Seek medical attention immediately if the blood spurts from the wound, or if it will not stop bleeding after 10 minutes of direct pressure.

Topical—Apply 1 to 2 drops of geranium, cypress, helichrysum, or lavender near the wound every 5 minutes until bleeding stops.

Other—Apply direct pressure to the wound.

Blisters

Topical—Apply 1 to 3 drops of lavender, German Chamomile, myrrh, or helichrysum to the blister several times daily.

Blisters (Fever)

Topical—Apply 1 drop of melaleuca (tea tree), clove, or rosemary to the blister several times daily.

Bloating

Oral—Take 1 to 3 drops of peppermint, juniper, and/or fennel in a capsule, 2 times daily.

Blood Clot

Abnormal blood clots can be a medical emergency and lead to a stroke, heart attack, or other serious conditions. Only use this protocol in conjunction with Western medical options and with approval from a physician.

Topical—Massage 4 drops of lavender to the bottoms of the feet up to 3 times daily. Apply 1 to 3 drops of cistus, lemon, orange, and helichrysum to the affected area, 3 to 5 times daily.

Oral—Take 2 capsules with 3 drops each of cistus, helichrysum, orange, grapefruit, and lemon, 2 times daily.

Boils

Topical—Apply 1 to 2 drops of lavender, frankincense, myrrh, peppermint, or melaleuca (tea tree), several times daily.

Bone Spurs

Topical—Apply 1 drop each of eucalyptus, myrtle, pine, lavender, tsuga, oregano, and peppermint to affected area, 2 to 3 times daily. Alternately, apply 2 to 5 drops of wintergreen, balsam fir, or cypress to affected area, 2 to 4 times daily.

Brain Injury

Only use this protocol in conjunction with Western medical options and with approval from a physician.

Topical—Apply 1 to 2 drops each of frankincense, vetiver, cedarwood, sandalwood, and helichrysum to the base of the skull and back of the neck, 3 to 5 times daily. Apply 2 drops each of black spruce, blue tansy, and frankincense to the bottom of the feet, 2 to 3 times daily. When the person recovers enough, apply 3 to 5 drops of oregano, thyme, basil, cypress, wintergreen, marjoram, and peppermint (layered in that order, 1 at a time) to the spine and massage into back on either side of the spine, 2 times weekly.

Oral—Take a capsule filled with 3 drops each of frankincense, vetiver, sandalwood, cedarwood, and helichrysum, 1 to 3 times daily. Alternately, place 1 drop of each oil on the tongue, 1 to 3 times daily.

Brittle Bones

Topical—Apply 1 to 3 drops of wintergreen, helichrysum, and balsam fir to affected bones, 2 to 3 times daily. Women apply 1 to 3 drops of clary sage to the forehead or carotid arteries, 3 times daily. Men apply 3 drops of blue spruce to the feet, 3 times daily.

Broken Bones

Broken bones require more than essential oils. Seek medical attention to have the bone set and casted. This protocol is intended to help relieve pain and encourage normal healing of bones. It should be followed for the duration that the cast is on, applying oils for 3 weeks before resting 1 week, then repeating the application process.

Topical—Apply 3 drops each of balsam fir, cypress, helichrysum, lemongrass, and wintergreen to the area, 2 to 4 times daily.

Oral—Take a capsule filled with 5 drops each of balsam fir, copaiba, and frankincense, 1 to 3 times daily.

Other—Do not move the person if at all possible; this could make the injury worse. Apply a splint above and below the fracture sites if you are trained how to do so.

Bronchitis

Topical—Apply 3 to 5 drops of eucalyptus, ginger, myrtle, and/or copaiba to the chest as needed. Apply 3 to 5 drops each of oregano and 1 drop of thyme to the bottoms of the feet, 2 to 4 times daily.

Inhalation—Place 2 to 3 drops each of eucalyptus, myrtle, and copaiba in half cup of hot water in bowl, cover head and bowl with towel and inhale 3 to 6 times daily. To improve outcome, hold your breath for as long as possible during the inhalation then breathe out slowly.

Oral—Take 1 capsule filled with 3 drops carrier oil and 2 drops each of clove, cinnamon, lemon, oregano, and rosemary, 1 to 3 times daily.

Brucellosis

Oral—Take a capsule filled with 3 drops each of cinnamon, lemon, peppermint, marjoram, and 1 drop of nutmeg, 1 to 3 times daily.

Topical—Apply 3 drops each of lemon and peppermint to the spine as needed for fever. Apply 1 to 2 drops each of basil, marjoram, and ginger to sore muscles as needed.

Bruise/Bumps

Topical—Apply 2 to 4 drops of helichrysum, blue tansy, lavender, and/or frankincense to the bruise and surrounding area, several times daily (it is best to begin application directly after a blow that may cause a bruise).

Bunions

Topical—Apply 1 to 2 drops of lemon, wintergreen, and pine to the bunion, several times daily.

Burns

Other—Cool the area in cold water for several minutes. Do not use ice.

Topical—Apply 2 to 3 drops of lavender, melaleuca (tea tree), or German chamomile to the burn every 15 minutes until pain subsides, and then apply every two hours or as necessary until healing is complete.

Bursitis

Topical—Apply 2 to 4 drops each of wintergreen, balsam fir, and cypress to affected area, 3 to 5 times daily.

Calcific Tendinitis

Topical—Apply 2 drops each of cypress, balsam fir, eucalyptus, and wintergreen and 1 drop each of grapefruit, lemongrass, and lemon to and widely around the affected area, 2 to 3 times daily.

Oral—For difficult calcification, take a capsule filled with 8 drops of lemon, 2 drops each of frankincense and balsam fir, and 1 drop of wintergreen, 1 to 2 times daily.

Calluses

Topical—Apply 1 to 2 drops of oregano, lavender, or frankincense to the area, 2 to 3 times daily.

Cancer (Enriched Frankincense, And Disclaimer)

Both H.K. Lin, PhD, and Mahmoud Suhail, MD—who have extensive experience working with frankincense and cancer—recommend using "enriched" **Boswellia sacra** for cancer. Enriched frankincense is simply frankincense bottles that have been left open to allow the lighter chemical compounds to evaporate out, leaving the heavier chemical compounds. The bottle is allowed to evaporate until only 20 percent of the oil remains. According to Dr. Lin, this makes **Boswellia sacra** 10 times more potent. Because cancer is a devastating disease, aggressive action is often necessary to correct it. Large oral doses are frequently suggested and may be difficult to take immediately; therefore, it is prudent to work up to the recommended dosage to allow the body to adjust.

You may start with 1 quarter of the dosage, then work to half, and then to the full dose over a period of several days to a couple weeks. The same applies for orange oil when indicated. The average essential oil contains from 20 to 40 drops of essential oil per 1 mL. This figure can be used as a guide for dosing, but oils vary significantly based on their specific gravity, so it is not perfect. In general, 30 drops per milliliter is a good average.

Disclaimer: *Cancer is one of the most common life-threatening illnesses that affects up to half of us during our lifetime. You should never attempt to treat it alone. Ideally you will work closely with your physician and determine the best course of action that will lead you to healing. This partnership provides the greatest possibility of successful treatment and survival.*

Cancer (Bladder)

Oral—Take 0.018 to 0.045 ml of enriched frankincense or frankincense per pound of body weight (for example, a 150-pound person would take 2.7 to 6.75 ml daily) in 3 to 6 divided doses throughout the day with food for 21 days, then rest for 7 days, and restart regimen if necessary. Take a capsule with 15 drops of orange oil, 3 to 6 times daily. Take an additional capsule with 10 drops of sandalwood oil, 2 times daily.

Other—Intermittent fasting (only consuming water) for 24 hours, 2 times weekly, or 48 hours once weekly. Alternately, some practitioners recommend fasting for

30-plus days drinking only vegetable and fruit juices. Make sure they don't have added sugar.

Topical—Apply 3 to 5 drops each of sandalwood, basil, and orange to the affected area up to 6 times daily.

Cancer (Bone)

Oral—Take 0.018 to 0.045 ml of enriched frankincense or frankincense per pound of body weight (for example, a 150-pound person would take 2.7 to 6.75 ml daily) in 3 to 6 divided doses throughout the day with food for 21 days, then rest for 7 days, and restart regimen if necessary. Take a capsule with 15 drops of orange oil, 3 to 6 times daily. Take an additional capsule with 10 drops of clove oil, 2 times daily.

Other—Intermittent fasting (only consuming water) for 24 hours, 2 times weekly, or 48 hours once weekly. Alternately, some practitioners recommend fasting for 30-plus days drinking only vegetable and fruit juices. Make sure they don't have added sugar.

Topical—Apply 3 to 5 drops each of clove, tsuga, and frankincense over the bladder area up to 6 times daily.

Cancer (Brain)

Topical—Apply 1 to 3 drops each of lemongrass, lemon, oregano, German chamomile, and thyme to the base of the skull and behind the ears, 3 to 6 times daily.

Oral—Take 0.018 to 0.045 ml of enriched frankincense or frankincense per pound of body weight (for example, a 150-pound person would take 2.7 to 6.75 ml daily) in 3 to 6 divided doses throughout the day with food for 21 days, then rest for 7 days, and restart regimen if necessary. Take 0.02 to 0.067 ml (about 3 to 10 ml for a 150-pound person) of orange per pound of body weight in 3 divided doses with food daily for 21 days, then rest for 7 days, and restart regimen if necessary.

Other—Intermittent fasting (only consuming water) for 24 hours, 2 times weekly, or 48 hours once weekly. Alternately, some practitioners recommend fasting for 30-plus days drinking only vegetable and fruit juices. Make sure they don't have added sugar.

Cancer (Breast)

Topical—Rub copious amounts of frankincense, sandalwood, myrrh, blue spruce, and myrtle on breasts, several times daily.

Oral—Take 0.018 to 0.045 ml of enriched frankincense or frankincense per pound of body weight (for example, a 150-pound person would take 2.7 to 6.75 ml daily) in 3 to 6 divided doses throughout the day with food for 21 days, then rest for 7 days, and restart regimen if necessary. Take 0.02 to 0.067 ml (about 3 to 10 ml for a 150-pound person) of orange per pound of body weight in 3 divided doses with food daily for 21 days, then rest for 7 days, and restart regimen if necessary.

Other—Intermittent fasting (only consuming water) for 24 hours, 2 times weekly, or 48 hours once weekly. Alternately, some practitioners recommend fasting for 30-plus days drinking only vegetable and fruit juices. Make sure they don't have added sugar.

Cancer (Cervical)

Topical—Apply copious amounts of frankincense and tsuga over the pubic area, several times daily.

Oral—Take 0.018 to 0.045 ml of enriched frankincense or frankincense per pound of body weight (for example, a 150-pound person would take 2.7 to 6.75 ml daily) in 3 to 6 divided doses throughout the day with food for 21 days, then rest for 7 days, and restart regimen if necessary. Take 0.02 to 0.067 ml (about 3 to 10 ml for a 150-pound person) of orange per pound of body weight in 3 divided doses with food daily for 21 days, then rest for 7 days, and restart regimen if necessary.

Retention—Consider inserting 15 drops of frankincense and 5 drops of tsuga mixed with 1 tablespoon of carrier oil into the vagina on a tampon.

Other—Intermittent fasting (only consuming water) for 24 hours, 2 times weekly, or 48 hours once weekly. Alternately, some practitioners recommend fasting for

30-plus days drinking only vegetable and fruit juices. Make sure they don't have added sugar.

Cancer (Colon)

Topical—Apply copious amounts of frankincense and sandalwood over the lower abdomen, several times daily.

Oral—Take 0.018 to 0.045 ml of enriched frankincense or frankincense per pound of body weight (for example, a 150-pound person would take 2.7 to 6.75 ml daily) in 3 to 6 divided doses throughout the day with food for 21 days, then rest for 7 days, and restart regimen if necessary. Take 0.02 to 0.067 ml (about 3 to 10 ml for a 150-pound person) of orange per pound of body weight in 3 divided doses with food daily for 21 days, then rest for 7 days, and restart regimen if necessary.

Retention—Consider inserting 10 drops each of frankincense and sandalwood mixed with 30 to 50 drops of carrier oil into the rectum and retaining.

Other—Intermittent fasting (only consuming water) for 24 hours, 2 times weekly, or 48 hours once weekly; alternately, some practitioners recommend fasting for 30-plus days drinking only vegetable and fruit juices. Make sure they don't have added sugar.

Cancer (Gastric, Stomach)

Topical—Apply copious amounts of frankincense and sandalwood over the lower abdomen, several times daily.

Oral—Take 1 capsule filled with 5 to 10 drops of each listed oil—frankincense, clove, rosemary, ginger, and 2 drops of nutmeg—3 times daily for 21 days, then rest for 7 days, and restart regimen if necessary. Take 1 capsule with 5 drops each of lemongrass, basil, and cinnamon, once daily. Take 0.02 to 0.067 ml (about 3 to 10 ml for a 150-pound person) of orange per pound of body weight in 3 divided doses with food daily. If stomach irritation occurs, apply the oils topically over the stomach instead.

Other—Intermittent fasting (only consuming water) for 24 hours, 2 times weekly, or 48 hours once weekly. Alternately, some practitioners recommend fasting for 30-plus days drinking only vegetable and fruit juices. Make sure they don't have added sugar.

Cancer (Lung)

Topical—Apply copious amounts of frankincense, myrrh, and orange to the front and back of the ribs several times daily.

Oral—Take 0.018 to 0.045 ml of enriched frankincense or frankincense per pound of body weight (for example, a 150-pound person would take 2.7 to 6.75 ml daily) in 3 to 6 divided doses throughout the day with food for 21 days, then rest for 7 days, and restart regimen if necessary. Take 0.02 to 0.067 ml (about 3 to 10 ml for a 150-pound person) of orange per pound of body weight in 3 divided doses with food daily for 21 days, then rest for 7 days, and restart regimen if necessary.

Inhalation—Place 15 drops each of myrtle and eucalyptus in 3 inches of hot water that is not too hot to touch with your hand and cover head with towel to inhale every 2 hours.

Other—Intermittent fasting (only consuming water) for 24 hours, 2 times weekly, or 48 hours once weekly. Alternately, some practitioners recommend fasting for 30-plus days drinking only vegetable and fruit juices. Make sure they don't have added sugar.

Cancer (Oral)

Oral—First thing in the morning and on an empty stomach, add 2 drops each of clove, oregano, thyme and frankincense to 1 tablespoon of coconut oil; hold this mixture in the mouth and agitate regularly for 10 to 15 minutes—or until the oil thickens—then spit out (**DO NOT SWALLOW** as this procedure may pull toxins from the oral cavity). Repeat this procedure up to 3 times daily on an empty stomach. Take 0.018 to 0.045 ml of enriched frankincense or frankincense per pound of body weight (for example, a 150-pound person would take 2.7 to 6.75 ml daily) in 3 to 6 divided doses throughout the day with food for 21 days, then rest for 7 days and restart regimen if necessary; take 0.02 to 0.067 ml (about 3 to 10 ml for a 150-pound person) of orange per pound of body weight in 3 divided doses with food daily for 21 days, then rest for 7 days, and restart regimen if necessary.

Other—Intermittent fasting (only consuming water) for 24 hours, 2 times weekly, or 48 hours once weekly; alternately, some practitioners recommend fasting for 30-plus days drinking only vegetable and fruit juices. Make sure they don't have added sugar.

Cancer (Ovarian)

Topical—Heavily dilute and apply 2 to 4 drops each of thyme, sandalwood, frankincense, geranium, and cypress to the lower abdominal region area, 3 to 5 times daily.

Oral—Take 0.018 to 0.045 ml of enriched frankincense or frankincense per pound of body weight (for example, a 150-pound person would take 2.7 to 6.75 ml daily) in 3 to 6 divided doses throughout the day with food for 21 days, then rest for 7 days, and restart regimen if necessary. Take 0.02 to 0.067 ml (about 3 to 10 ml for a 150-pound person) of orange per pound of body weight in 3 divided doses with food daily for 21 days, then rest for 7 days, and restart regimen if necessary.

Other—Intermittent fasting (only consuming water) for 24 hours, 2 times weekly or 48 hours once weekly. Alternately, some practitioners recommend fasting for 30-plus days drinking only vegetable and fruit juices. Make sure they don't have added sugar.

Cancer (Pancreatic)

Topical—Apply copious amounts of frankincense, myrrh, and orange to the middle part of the left side of the back several times daily.

Oral—Take 0.018 to 0.045 ml of enriched frankincense or frankincense per pound of body weight (for example, a 150-pound person would take 2.7 to 6.75 ml daily) in 3 to 6 divided doses throughout the day with food for 21 days, then rest for 7 days, and restart regimen if necessary. Take 0.02 to 0.067 ml (about 3 to 10 ml for a 150-pound person) of orange per pound of body weight in 3 divided doses with food daily for 21 days, then rest for 7 days, and restart regimen if necessary.

Other—Intermittent fasting (only consuming water) for 24 hours, 2 times weekly, or 48 hours once weekly. Alternately, some practitioners recommend fasting for 30-plus days drinking only vegetable and fruit juices. Make sure they don't have added sugar.

Cancer (Prostate)

Topical—Apply copious amounts of frankincense, sandalwood, and myrrh over the lower abdomen several times daily.

Oral—Take 0.018 to 0.045 ml of enriched frankincense or frankincense per pound of body weight (for example, a 150-pound person would take 2.7 to 6.75 ml daily) in 3 to 6 divided doses throughout the day with food for 21 days, then rest for 7 days, and restart regimen if necessary. Take .067 ml (about 10 ml for a 150-pound person) of orange per pound of body weight in 3 divided doses with food daily for 21 days, then rest for 7 days, and restart regimen if necessary.

Retention—Consider inserting 10 drops each of frankincense and sandalwood mixed with 1 tablespoon drops of carrier oil into the rectum and retaining.

Other—Intermittent fasting (only consuming water) for 24 hours, 2 times weekly, or 48 hours once weekly. Alternately, some practitioners recommend fasting for 30-plus days drinking only vegetable and fruit juices. Make sure they don't have added sugar.

Cancer (Skin)

Topical—Apply copious amounts of frankincense, melaleuca (tea tree), and 1 of the following: balsam fir or sandalwood to affected area several times daily

Oral—Take 0.018 to 0.045 ml of enriched frankincense or frankincense per pound of body weight (for example a 150-pound person would take 2.7 to 6.75 ml daily) in 3 to 6 divided doses throughout the day with food for 21 days, then rest for 7 days, and restart regimen if necessary. Take .067 ml (about 10 ml for a 150-pound person) of orange per pound of body weight in 3 divided doses with food daily for 21 days, then rest for 7 days, and restart regimen if necessary.

Other—Intermittent fasting (only consuming water) for 24 hours, 2 times weekly, or 48 hours once weekly. Alternately, some practitioners recommend fasting for 30-plus days drinking only vegetable and fruit juices. Make sure they don't have added sugar.

Cancer (Testicular)

Topical—Mix 10 drops each of frankincense and blue spruce in 2 teaspoons of carrier oil and apply to the testicles, 2 times daily.

Oral—Take 0.018 to 0.045 ml of enriched frankincense or frankincense per pound of body weight (for example, a 150-pound person would take 2.7 to 6.75 ml daily) in 3 to 6 divided doses throughout the day with food for 21 days, then rest for 7 days, and restart regimen if necessary. Take 0.02 to 0.067 ml (about 3 to 10 ml for a 150-pound person) of orange per pound of body weight in 3 divided doses with food daily for 21 days, then rest for 7 days, and restart regimen if necessary.

Other—Intermittent fasting (only consuming water) for 24 hours, 2 times weekly, or 48 hours once weekly. Alternately, some practitioners recommend fasting for 30-plus days drinking only vegetable and fruit juices. Make sure they don't have added sugar.

Cancer (Thyroid)

Topical—Apply 1 drop each of frankincense, balsam fir, myrtle, German chamomile, and nutmeg to the neck over the thyroid, 3 to 6 times daily.

Oral—Take 0.018 to 0.045 ml of enriched frankincense or frankincense per pound of body weight (for example, a 150-pound person would take 2.7 to 6.75 ml daily) in 3 to 6 divided doses throughout the day with food for 21 days, then rest for 7 days, and restart regimen if necessary. Take 0.02 to 0.067 ml (about 3 to 10 ml for a 150-pound person) of orange per pound of body weight in 3 divided doses with food daily for 21 days, then rest for 7 days, and restart regimen if necessary.

Other—Intermittent fasting (only consuming water) for 24 hours, 2 times weekly, or 48 hours once weekly. Alternately, some practitioners recommend fasting for 30-plus days drinking only vegetable and fruit juices. Make sure they don't have added sugar.

Cancer (Uterine)

Topical—Heavily dilute and apply 2 to 4 drops each of thyme, sandalwood, frankincense, geranium, and cypress to the lower abdominal region area, 3 to 5 times daily.

Oral—Take 0.018 to 0.045 ml of enriched frankincense or frankincense per pound of body weight (for example, a 150-pound person would take 2.7 to 6.75 ml daily) in 3 to 6 divided doses throughout the day with food for 21 days, then rest for 7 days, and restart regimen if necessary. Take 0.02 to 0.067 ml (about 3 to 10 ml for a 150-pound person) of orange per pound of body weight in 3 divided doses with food daily for 21 days, then rest for 7 days, and restart regimen if necessary.

Other—Intermittent fasting (only consuming water) for 24 hours, 2 times weekly or 48 hours once weekly. Alternately, some practitioners recommend fasting for 30-plus days drinking only vegetable and fruit juices. Make sure they don't have added sugar.

Cancer (Vaginal, Vulvar)

Topical—Heavily dilute and apply 2 to 4 drops each of sandalwood, frankincense, geranium, and cypress to the vulva and labia area, 3 to 5 times daily. Apply 8 to 10 drops of orange oil to the bottoms of the feet, 2 to 3 times daily. Apply more geranium and helichrysum as the area begins to heal to prevent scarring.

Oral—Take 0.018 to 0.045 ml of enriched frankincense or frankincense per pound of body weight (for example, a 150-pound person would take 2.7 to 6.75 ml daily) in 3 to 6 divided doses throughout the day with food for 21 days.

Other—Intermittent fasting (only consuming water) for 24 hours, 2 times weekly, or 48 hours once weekly. Alternately, some practitioners recommend fasting for 30-plus days drinking only vegetable and fruit juices. Make sure they don't have added sugar.

Candida

Topical—Apply 1 to 3 drops each of lemongrass, clove, eucalyptus, lavender, and melaleuca (tea tree) to the bottoms of the feet, 2 times daily.

Oral—Take 3 drops each of oregano, lemongrass, lavender, and lemon in a capsule, 3 times daily.

Canker Sores

Topical—Apply 1 drop of 1 or more of clove, lemon, melaleuca (tea tree), and/or peppermint directly to the canker sore several times daily. Rotating which oils are used will increase effectiveness.

Carpal Tunnel Syndrome

Topical—Apply a combination of lemongrass, marjoram, peppermint, cypress, and wintergreen to affected area, several times daily.

Oral—For added support, take a capsule filled with 4 drops each of frankincense, copaiba, balsam fir, and lemongrass, 2 to 3 times daily.

Cataracts

Topical—Apply lemongrass, frankincense, and lavender mixed with a little carrier oil widely around the orbit of the eye at night before going to bed.

Oral—Take 1 capsule filled with 5 drops each of frankincense, lavender, and lemongrass, 2 times daily.

Cavities

See your dentist to repair the cavity.

Topical—Apply clove and cinnamon oil to tooth (may require dilution), 3 times daily.

Celiac Disease

Oral—Take a capsule filled with 4 drops of lemon, and ginger, and 1 drop each of cinnamon, grapefruit, fennel, and peppermint, 3 times daily, preferably before each meal.

Cellulitis

Topical—Apply 1 drop each of helichrysum, lavender, melaleuca (tea tree), eucalyptus, and thyme to the affected area, 2 to 3 times daily.

Chapped Skin

Topical—Apply 2 to 3 drops of lavender and/or myrrh and German chamomile to affected area as often as needed.

Charcot Foot (Neuropathic Arthropathy)

Topical—Apply 8 to 10 drops of orange oil to the bottoms of the feet, 2 times daily. Massage 4 drops each of blue spruce, cypress, balsam fir, and vetiver to the top of the feet, 2 to 4 times daily. For wounds, apply 1 to 2 drops each of frankincense, copaiba, cedarwood, and lavender to the wound, several times daily.

Cherry Angioma

Topical—Apply a few drops of a mixture containing equal portions of frankincense, cistus, lemongrass, German chamomile, lavender, and orange in 4 teaspoons of carrier oil to the affected area, several times daily.

Oral —Take a capsule filled with 5 drops each of frankincense, lemongrass, and orange, 2 to 3 times daily.

Chicken Pox

Topical—Mix 5 drops each of melaleuca (tea tree), lavender, lemongrass, and German chamomile with equal parts carrier oil and apply to spots, 3 times daily.

Oral—Take a capsule with 3 drops each of lemongrass, oregano, and lemon, 2 to 3 times daily.

Chilblains

Topical—Apply 1 drop each of German chamomile, lavender, and cypress to the affected area, 1 to 3 times daily. Alternately, add 1 drop of each to each application of lotion.

Cholera

Oral—Take a capsule filled with 3 drops each of oregano and cinnamon, and 1 drop each of eucalyptus, melaleuca (tea tree), and thyme up to 4 times daily.

Other—Drink plenty of water with electrolytes to replenish what has been lost through diarrhea.

Chronic Fatigue

Topical—Apply frankincense, sandalwood, and cedarwood to the base of the skull, brain stem, and head, 2 to 4 times daily.

Inhalation—Place 2 drops of peppermint in 1 palm, rub together with other palm, and cup over nose and mouth to inhale as often as necessary.

Oral—Take a capsule filled with 3 drops each of lemongrass, myrrh, and German chamomile, 2 times daily.

Chronic Obstructive Pulmonary Disease (Copd)

Topical—Apply 3 to 5 drops of eucalyptus, myrtle, cedarwood, peppermint and/or copaiba to the chest as needed. Apply 3 to 5 drops each of oregano and 1 drop of thyme to the bottoms of the feet, 2 to 4 times daily.

Inhalation—Place 1 to 2 drops of eucalyptus, rosemary, myrtle, and peppermint in 3 inches of hot water that is not too hot to touch with your hand, and cover head with towel to inhale, 1 or 2 times daily.

Oral—Take 1 capsule filled with 2 drops each of pine, orange, lemon, eucalyptus, and ginger up to 3 times daily.

Circulation, Poor

Topical—Apply 1 to 2 drops each of cypress, helichrysum, and cedarwood to the area of poor circulation, 3 to 5 times daily.

Oral—Take a capsule filled with 3 drops each of lemongrass, cypress, clove, and cinnamon, morning and evening.

Diabetes

Topical—Apply 1 to 3 drops each of cinnamon, lemongrass, fennel, and copaiba to the bottoms of the feet, particularly the pancreas VitaFlex point on the outer edge of the left foot about midway down, 2 to 4 times daily.

Oral—Take 1 capsule with 2 drops each of cinnamon, fennel, lemongrass, and grapefruit, morning and evening.

Diarrhea

Oral—Take a capsule with 3 drops each of peppermint and fennel, 1 to 3 times daily, or until diarrhea is relieved.

Topical—Apply 1 to 3 drops of peppermint and fennel over the abdomen every hour or until diarrhea is relieved.

Other—Drink plenty of water to replenish lost fluids.

Distal Renal Tubular Acidosis

Oral—Take a capsule filled with 7 drops of lemon and 3 drops of juniper, 2 to 3 times daily.

Topical—Apply 2 to 3 drops of pine over the kidney area on the back, 3 times daily.

Diverticulitis

Oral—Take 1 capsule filled with 2 drops each of oregano, peppermint, nutmeg, cypress, fennel, and marjoram, 2 to 3 times daily.

Topical—Apply oregano, peppermint, nutmeg, cypress, fennel, and marjoram over the abdomen, 2 to 3 times daily.

Dizziness

Inhalation—Place 1 drop each of peppermint and cypress in 1 palm, rub together with other palm, and cup hands over mouth and nose to inhale as often as necessary.

Topical—Apply peppermint, frankincense, or cypress to the temples, back of the neck and shoulders.

Dopamine Deficiency

Topical—Apply 1 to 2 drops of geranium, eucalyptus, and clary sage behind and underneath the ears, 1 to 3 times daily.

Inhalation—Place 1 drop of geranium, lemon, and clary sage on a tissue and inhale as needed. Refresh tissue up to 3 times daily.

Dry Skin

Topical—Apply lavender, myrrh, or German chamomile to affected area as often as needed.

Dupuytren's Contracture

Topical—Massage 1 drop each of cistus, basil, marjoram, vetiver, and frankincense to the affected area several times daily.

Dysesthesia (Cutaneous)

Topical—Apply 1 drops each of vetiver, blue spruce, peppermint, juniper, German chamomile, and helichrysum to the area, 2 to 4 times daily.

Oral—Take a capsule with 5 drops of helichrysum and 2 drops each of vetiver, copaiba, and lavender, 1 to 3 times daily.

Dysentery

Seek medical attention if symptoms are severe or last longer than a few days.

Oral—Take 1 capsule with 4 drops each of peppermint, lemon, and oregano, 2 to 3 times daily.

Topical—Apply 1 to 3 drops of peppermint, wintergreen, fennel, or oregano to abdomen, 2 to 3 times daily.

Ear Infection

Topical—Apply 1 to 2 drops each of lavender and melaleuca (tea tree) around the ear and on the fleshy part of the ear every 30 minutes until pain subsides, and then apply every 2 hours. Apply 1 to 2 drops each of oregano, cinnamon, clove, rosemary, and lemon to the bottom of the feet every 30 minutes until pain subsides, and then every 2 to 4 hours for the next 24 hours.

Other—Apply 1 drop of melaleuca (tea tree) to a cotton ball and place inside ear, refresh every 30 minutes until pain diminishes, and then refresh every 2 hours; leave a fresh cotton ball in overnight.

Ear Mites

Topical—Apply 2 to 3 drops each of eucalyptus and melaleuca (tea tree) around the ear and on the fleshy part of the ear, 3 to 5 times daily.

Other—Apply 1 drop of melaleuca (tea tree) and eucalyptus to a cotton ball and place inside ear, and then refresh every hour; leave a fresh cotton ball in overnight.

Earache

Topical—Apply 1 to 2 drops each of peppermint and lavender around the ear and on the fleshy part of the ear every 30 minutes until pain subsides, and then apply every 2 hours. Apply 1 to 2 drops each of oregano, cinnamon, clove, rosemary or melaleuca (tea tree), and lemon to the bottom of the feet every 30 minutes until pain subsides, and then every 2 to 4 hours for the next 24 hours.

Other—Apply 1 drop of melaleuca (tea tree) to a cotton ball and place inside ear, refresh every 30 minutes until pain diminishes, and then refresh every 2 hours; leave a fresh cotton ball in overnight.

Conclusion

Essential oils have a numerous amount of benefits and they can certainly help you if you're looking to take care of some physical issues.

They can help with bodily issues, issues with beauty, and if you're sick, this can be the go-to item to help you out. They are certainly worth the money, and it's definitely something you should try to get into.

For many people, having essential oils can help to change your life. If you're worried about what your body might do with essential oils, always make sure to diffuse it. It's best that you don't ingest them unless you know for a fact that it is safe to do so. But, if you want to get into using these you can try new means in order to accomplish various tasks with them. There are so many uses, probably hundreds of them, and they can be a great way to engage in preventative medicine. You also can use them around your home, and it will get your place smelling pretty great too.

www.ingramcontent.com/pod-product-compliance
Lightning Source LLC
Chambersburg PA
CBHW052011070526
44584CB00016B/1700